SPHINX

SPHINX

History of a Monument

CHRISTIANE ZIVIE-COCHE

translated from the French by
DAVID LORTON

Cornell University Press
Ithaca & London

First published 2002 by Cornell University Press

Printed in the United States of America

Library of Congress Cataloging-in-Publication Data

Zivie-Coche, Christiane.
    Sphinx : history of a moument / Christiane Zivie-Coche ; translated from the French By David Lorton.
        p. cm.
Includes bibliographical references and index.
    ISBN 0-8014-3962-0 (cloth : alk. paper)
    1. Great Sphinx (Egypt)—History. I. Title.
    DT62.S7 Z58 2002
932—dc21

                                                            2002005494

Cloth printing   10 9 8 7 6 5 4 3 2 1

TO YOU

PIEDRA en la piedra, el hombre, dónde estuvo?

—*Canto general,* Pablo Neruda

Contents

Acknowledgments

Agnès Viénot and Guy Stavridès originated this project, and I am grateful to them for having led me to rediscover this much-surveyed site.

I must express my debt to Jacques J. Clère, who long ago gave me photographs of the stelae from Giza in the Cairo Museum.

Last, I would like to thank Bernhard Kendler, Executive Editor, and Cornell University Press and David Lorton, Egyptologist and translator of this volume.

Translator's Note

In this book, the following conventions have been followed in the citations from ancient texts:

Parentheses ( ) enclose words or brief explanations that have been added for clarity.

Square brackets [ ] enclose words that have been restored in a lacuna.

An ellipsis . . . indicates that a word or words in the original text have been omitted in the citation.

An ellipsis in square brackets [. . .] indicates the presence of a lacuna for which no restoration has been attempted.

There is no single set of conventions for the English rendering of ancient Egyptian and modern Arabic personal and place names. Most of the names mentioned in this book occur in a standard reference work, John Baines and Jaromir Malek, *Cultural Atlas of Ancient Egypt* (New York, 2000), and the renderings here follow those in that volume. The principal exception is the omission of the typographical sign for *ayin*; this consonant does not exist in English, and it was felt that its inclusion would serve only as a distraction to the reader.

In chapter 7, the passage from Pliny the Elder is derived from D. E. Eichholz, *Pliny: Natural History* (Cambridge, Mass., 1962), pp. 59–65. The question from Diodorus is from E. Murphy, *Diodorus on Egypt* (Jefferson, N. C., 1985), p. 84. As noted in the bibliography, the Greek inscriptions cited at the end of the chapter are taken from a French translation, here rendered into English.

Chronology*

* Down to the eighth century, the dates are approximate.

SPHINX

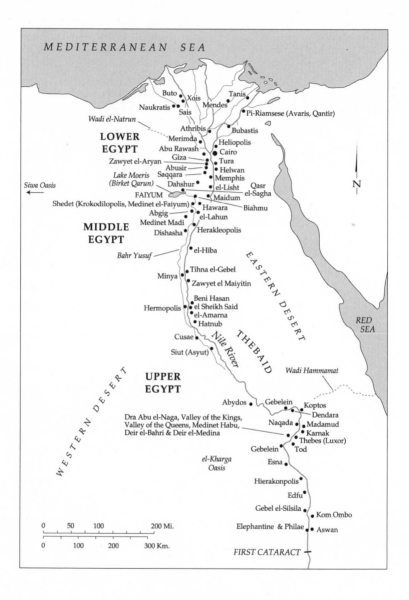

MEDITERRANEAN SEA

Buto
Xois
Naukratis
Sais
Mendes
Tanis
Pi-Riamsese (Avaris, Qantir)

Wadi el-Natrun

LOWER
EGYPT

Athribis
Bubastis
Merimda
Heliopolis
Abu Rawash
Cairo
Zawyet el-Aryan
Giza
Tura
Abusir
Helwan
Saqqara
Memphis
Lake Moeris
(Birket Qarun)
Dahshur
el-Lisht
Qasr
el-Sagha

Siwa Oasis

FAIYUM
Maidum

Shedet (Krokodilopolis, Medinet el-Faiyum)
Hawara
Biahmu
Abgig
el-Lahun
Medinet Madi
MIDDLE
EGYPT
Dishasha
Herakleopolis

Bahr Yusuf
el-Híba

Minya
Tihna el-Gebel
Zawyet el Maiyitin

Beni Hasan
el Sheikh Said
Hermopolis
el-Amarna
Hatnub

EASTERN DESERT

RED
SEA

Cusae
Nile River

Siut (Asyut)

THEBAID

UPPER
EGYPT

Wadi Hammamat

WESTERN DESERT

Abydos
Gebelein
Koptos
Dendara
Dra Abu el-Naga, Valley of the Kings,
Valley of the Queens, Medinet Habu,
Deir el-Bahri & Deir el-Medina
Naqada
Madamud
Karnak
Thebes (Luxor)
Gebelein
Tod

el-Kharga
Oasis

Esna

Hierakonpolis

Edfu

Gebel el-Silsila
Kom Ombo
Elephantine & Philae
Aswan

N

0   50   100   200 Mi.

0   100   200   300 Km.

FIRST CATARACT

Introduction

The image of the Sphinx is familiar—so familiar that we do not even have to call it the Sphinx of Giza. We see it on travel posters everywhere. A rainy day in a city in northern Europe: is the crowd in the subway tunnels dreaming about this Sphinx at the foot of the pyramids, under a relentlessly blue sky, along with a camel, a valiant beast calmly carrying a tourist on his ritual duty? We are evidently to believe it, because buses, with their air-conditioning and their sound systems, constantly disgorge their cargoes of visitors who stand silently before the Sphinx, gazing back through the millennia for a moment, before they plunge into the thicket of bazaars in the village of Nazlet el-Simman, a suburb of Cairo. A pilgrimage, like those made by ancient visitors to the site? Perhaps. The sometimes crude ex-votos with images of the god Harmakhis that were once sold in this very place are nowadays replaced by hideous alabaster idols and garishly painted imitation papyri of banana leaf—more junk to put on a shelf back home. When night falls and the wind blows in from the desert, the site is swept by spotlights of red and green—the Sound and Light show. Amenophis II's bow is bent, his arrow hits its target, and we hear the gallop of his horses in the darkness. With a deep voice, Harmakhis addresses the young Tuthmosis as he sleeps. Bonaparte utters his fateful sentence. The end! And far away, in America, a pyramid-shaped casino with a sphinx in front of it gazing up at the sky triumphantly sports the name Luxor Las Vegas. Egyptomania reaps its harvest.

However hideous these modern cultural symbols may be, such Egyptianizing trash abounds—pyramids, sphinxes, obelisks, Nefertiti, King Tut, Ramesses II, Abu Simbel, Cleopatra. And like Marcel Duchamp's Mona Lisa with her marvelous mustache, the Sphinx must sometimes sport a bowler, thanks to Magritte.

Saint Harmakhis, protect us! Nothing stops us from going back to Giza to dream. The foggy, damp dawn is conducive to solitude, as is midday, though the white-hot sun is fearsome. And when the floodlights are off at night, the black profile of the human-headed lion stirs up an inexpressible emotion. To write, then: not to smash an old idol, but rather to lend it some substance. This literally fabulous being dates back to the Old Kingdom, to the reign of Chephren, who had it sculpted in his own image. We shall attempt to determine what role it played, but in the process, we shall shatter too widespread and long-lived an opinion. If the plateau of Giza—with its pyramids and Sphinx, counted by the Greeks among the Seven Wonders of the World because of the pyramid of Cheops and recognized today by UNESCO as part of the common heritage of humanity—is so famous, it is because of these sumptuous and unequaled tombs that testify to the past. But the other side of the coin is that these monuments have completely obscured the subsequent history of the site. Today we can study all the documentation that has been recovered—and it is highly instructive, albeit less stunning than the pyramids—and follow the step-by-step evolution of this site over nearly three thousand years. In Egypt, this is not a unique case, though such examples are uncommon. What became of this great cemetery after the fall of the Old Kingdom? What role was conferred on the Sphinx when it was rediscovered in the New Kingdom? How did it figure in the religious changes that marked the first millennium B.C.E.? Paradoxically, the mystery associated with the Sphinx has impeded development of a literature comparable to the ubiquitous para-Egyptological accounts. But I shall try to reveal the other side of the picture, to enable us to see behind the scenes of a history filled with twists and turns. I shall begin by situating the Great Sphinx in a larger context. Sphinxes are legion in Egypt—what is so special about this one? What is its relationship to all those others? We shall review the history of the excavations that have been conducted at the site of the Sphinx, which will tell us what was seen in the past and what has been destroyed; the records left by earlier excavators furnish researchers today with the evidence that our predecessors dug up from the ground. After that, we shall take a stroll around the monument itself, scrutinizing its special features and analyzing the changes it experienced in the course of its history. From there, the evidence linked to the statue will enable us to trace its evolution, from its conception by Chephren through its rehabilitation during the New Kingdom, when it was a popular destination for pilgrims, to its integration into a new religious vision of the pyramid plateau in the first millennium, and down to the worship it received in the first centuries of our own era, when Egyptians, Greeks, and Romans mingled together in devotion to this colossus, illustrious witness to a past that was already more than two millennia old.

I

Sphinx—Sphinxes

This book is devoted to an archetypal figure: the Great Sphinx of Giza, as it is habitually called to specify its location (Figure 1). It is unique in its colossal size, in its character as a statue carved in rock, in its intent, and in the transformations it experienced. Yet despite its special nature, it is but one of a category of Egyptian statues well represented in sculpture in the round, one of many sphinx statues. An exhaustive study of these images would be beyond our purpose in these pages, but we must make a brief account of them to assign the Sphinx of Giza its proper place among these many examples. Let us begin by adopting a minimal definition of an Egyptian sphinx, which has many iconographic variations. Doing so will enable us to summarize the figure's history before reflecting on its designation, its meaning, and its function. The Egyptian sphinx is a hybrid composed of a lion's body and a human head, a royal figure wearing the *nemes* headdress specific to monarchs, and usually provided with a short false beard, another attribute of royalty. Originally, and for a long time thereafter, it took the form of a recumbent animal, with its forelegs stretched out and separate from each other. But some sphinxes were depicted as walking on all fours, and, more rarely, some were depicted as seated. These sphinxes were masculine, though from the New Kingdom on, there were female sphinxes representing queens, inspired by the male sphinxes that depicted pharaohs.

The sphinx appeared relatively late in Egyptian iconography. Though

4

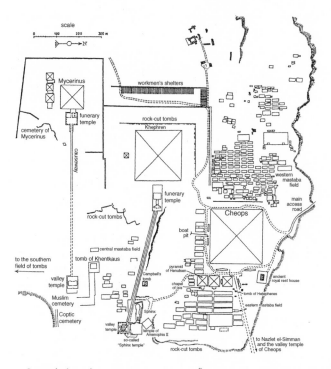

Figure 1. General plan of Giza. From *Lexikon der Ägyptologie*. Reproduced by permission of the publisher.

the predynastic palettes bear representations of fabulous animals, they use lions and not sphinxes to evoke the power of royalty. This lion symbolism, which dates back to the earliest eras, endured throughout the historical period; lions characterized the sovereign power of the pharaoh, which was also embodied by the image of the sphinx, though in a different manner. The mixed form of the sphinx seems not to have been devised until Dynasty 4. A small limestone sphinx that some consider to be feminine has been attributed to Radjedef, Chephren's predecessor, who was buried at Abu Rawash. Because of its nemes, a beautiful quartzite head of this king, now in the Louvre, supposedly belonged to a sphinx. These two early examples are not convincing, however, in part because they are not intact, and in part because there are problems with regard to their date.

Sphinx

Then came Chephren, who commissioned the carving of the Sphinx in the rock of the plateau of Giza, on a scale that was never equaled though it was proportionate to the site. Scholars might logically expect smaller specimens to have been produced during the reign of this sovereign, who left behind a rich statuary, yet none exist. It has been suggested that the gates of his valley temple were flanked by sphinxes, but no traces of them exist.

Assuming that the Sphinx of Giza, a constitutive element of Chephren's funerary complex, was a sort of prototype of the sphinxes to come, scholars once hoped to find others in later funerary complexes, in particular those of Dynasties 5 and 6 at Abusir and Saqqara. Such was not the case, however. It is true that the latter monuments are badly preserved; their bas-reliefs have suffered, and an incomplete image sometimes interpreted as a sphinx might be only a lion or a griffin, which had the body of a lion and the head of a falcon. The statuary is also quite poor; a base with feline legs, which bears the name of Pepy I, could have belonged to a sphinx, but there is no certainty of this. This situation is surprising if we maintain an atemporal view of Egyptian civilization, which is often credited with an obsessive permanence of forms that to a careless observer quickly becomes sheer repetitiveness. Yet Egyptian art changed far more over time than is generally supposed, and there were fashions, as we might call them, that privileged a particular model in a particular historical period, without our being able to explain why. The Sphinx of Giza seems to be an extraordinary work by an architect of genius, who created a new archetype in the service of a mighty sovereign whose image he was eager to magnify. He apparently had no immediate imitator, which in no way means that the form was lost—indeed, quite the contrary.

The Middle Kingdom saw a veritable renaissance of sphinxes. This statue type was highly prized by the sovereigns of Dynasty 12, who lent them a particular and always recognizable style. These are the sphinxes that have long been called Hyksos, after the name of the Semitic people who settled in the north of the delta at the end of the Middle Kingdom. Only the face is human, while the *nemes* is replaced by a lion's mane and ears, features that have sometimes led the sphinxes to be called lions with human faces. Dating to Amenemhet III and then usurped in Dynasty 19, they ended by adorning the temple of Amun at Tanis in the first millen-

Figure 2. Blue faience sphinx depicting Amenophis III presenting jars of wine. The Metropolitan Museum of Art, Purchase, Lila Acheson Wallace Gift, 1972. (1972.125). Reproduced by permission of The Metropolitan Museum of Art.

nium. The large sphinx in the Louvre, probably sculpted at the end of the Middle Kingdom and later usurped, is from this site.

This type of royal representation continued regularly throughout the New Kingdom. Among the many examples we have, the alabaster sphinx of Memphis, which remains *in situ*, without doubt dates stylistically to the beginning of the New Kingdom; it is the largest known specimen after that of Giza. The New Kingdom models display a variety of poses that were previously unknown. In the round and in reliefs, recumbent sphinxes offer an object—Maat (the symbol of order) or jars of wine (Figure 2)—to a deity, or assume the posture of adoration. In these cases, the sphinxes are more "humanized," because the lion's forelegs have been replaced by human arms and hands. But even Akhenaten, who made a clean break with most of the traditional principles of religion and art, did not refuse to have himself represented in this manner. Another pose became rather common, mostly on bas-reliefs: the striding sphinx trampling its enemies, a triumphal representation of a pharaoh's might. In the same period, images of queens as sphinxes made their appearance and became numerous. Although these sometimes scarcely differed from the masculine archetype, in other cases they had a different hairstyle, along with wings and breasts that clearly indicated their gender. This phenomenon likely reflected a Near Eastern influence, which was felt from that time on in Egyptian art. The Late Period and the Ptolemaic era did not renounce the traditional representation of the king. We know, among others, examples from Dynasties 26 and 30: for instance, the *dromos*, the alley of sphinxes that led to the Serapeum, was undoubtedly erected under Nectanebo I.

One category remains distinct from the models already mentioned. They are hybrids somewhat unjustifiably classified as sphinxes; they have a lion's body and the head of a ram (hence the designation "criosphinx"), and they represent the god Amun. In another combination, the head is that of a falcon. These mixed animals are especially to be found in the *dromoi* leading up to the pylons of temples. Making their appearance in Dynasty 18 under Tutankhamun or Haremhab, they adorned, for example, the processional route connecting the temples of Amun and Mut at Karnak. This type was derived from the sphinx with its typical combination of an animal body and a human face. But the curious representations of the god Tutu, or Tithoes, known only from the Ptolemaic Period, retain the human features of the original sphinx. The inventors of this late avatar made it a pan-iconic entity. The striding animal, with its head in profile or in frontal view, has a tail in the form of a serpent, while serpents or crocodiles emerge from its body. These images are proof that in Egypt, no form was immutable, but could, quite the contrary, lend itself to free interpretation, both in form and meaning, even distancing itself considerably from its original *raison d'être*.

THE HYBRID NATURE OF THE SPHINX

Strictly speaking, the sphinx combines the body of a lion with the face of a man, and the transition is hidden by the diagonal of the headdress that connects the head to the body. Such is the case with the Sphinx at Giza. No one looking at a sphinx would dream of speaking of a monstrous being; the blending of forms is perfect. In fact, Egypt is the land of mixed or double beings *par excellence;* hybridization was practically second nature. Temple walls are covered with images of Thoth with his ibis head, Montu with that of a falcon, and Hathor with a human face and cow's ears, side by side with purely anthropomorphic deities like Ptah, Osiris, or Amun, or others with an entirely animal form.[1] Therein resides all the difference. These beings are deities, and with few exceptions, the combination is that of a human body topped by an animal head. The sphinx illustrates the opposite principle: an animal body and a human head. Only one other association of this type is found in Egyptian iconology, one that became popular beginning with the New Kingdom. It is the image of the *ba,* a life force that existed in every human and divine being. In the form of a bird with a human head, it is depicted as having left the human body after death. These two examples, which run counter to divine iconography, are to be placed in relation to the human world; even a pharaoh, who participated in the human and the divine realms, was both a human being and a hypostasis representative of the divine on earth, in imitation of Horus.

This dichotomy between the two kinds of hybrids, one much more common than the other, touches on the Egyptian concept of the divine and on the manner in which it was represented. The ancient approach to the divine was never unequivocal, which explains how a single deity had several forms in which he or she was incarnate, as human, animal, or combination. The thesis of a progressive anthropomorphization of deities, which is often invoked in the study of other polytheistic religions, is not applicable to Egypt. In fact, as time went by, more theriomorphic divine figures were worshiped; their worship was most widespread at the end of the native dynasties. The human form, though stereotyped in its representation, recalled the individuality of a being; the image of an animal suggested an entire species. By uniting the two, the Egyptians could feel that they were most closely approaching the possibility of making an image of divine essence. But it was only an image, for deities were only temporar-

---

[1] We must never lose sight of this rule of divine polymorphism, which has few exceptions, or of its converse corollary: the same animal form can be the image of entirely different deities.

ily incarnate in their images. The ancients did not worship idols, despite what the early Christians claimed as they destroyed the pagan statues.

What was symbolized by the opposite phenomenon of an animal body and a human head? The individual is represented by the face, the supreme representation of a human being. This face could be that of anyone, in the case of the *ba* bird; when we stand before a sphinx, however, the face is that of a king. The head wears a royal headdress, and it generally has a false beard. But this head is poised on the body of a lion, symbol of triumphant power and incarnation of a divine principle. Thus the king, by virtue of this animality, surpasses his human condition and participates in the divine. This relationship with animality as a sign of the divine is found in other attributes specific to the pharaoh. He is often provided with an animal's tail, and his titulary frequently contains the epithet Mighty Bull, which could be interpreted simply as a metaphor, but which in Egyptian usage was charged with the pregnant power of the word.

As to the question of how a sphinx, a lion with a human head, is a royal and not a divine image, the answer is clear. Inscriptions accompanying these statues or reliefs state the name of the king, who in certain cases is declared to be beloved of a specific deity. Based on this principle, new interpretations could be introduced over time: thus the existence of the criosphinx and that of Tithoes. But the most surprising and original was the reinterpretation of the Sphinx of Giza, image of Chephren, as a god named Haremakhet, "Horus-in-the-horizon." Harmakhis (the Greek form of the name) was a deity in his own right, before whom the distant successors of the pharaohs of Dynasty 4 came to pay homage. To understand such a radical change, we must situate it within the long history of Giza.

THE WORD SPHINX

First, we must deal with the name of the Sphinx and with terms for this image that scholars believe they have found in the Egyptian lexicon. Provided we add the word "Egyptian," there is no doubt what we mean when we utter the word "sphinx." Without the adjective, confusion threatens, for "sphinx" is a borrowing from the Greek language, in which it designates an entirely different entity. The word used in modern languages is simply a rendering of the Greek noun σφινξ, of feminine gender. In Greek, it designates the female monster who sowed fear in Boeotia, not far from the city of Thebes, and whom the legends about Oedipus have made universally famous. References to this terrifying being would be more appropriate in calling it a "sphinge," but the masculine form has always prevailed. Greeks visiting Egypt endowed some typically Egyptian realities with Greek terms that had only a distant relationship with them and which sometimes seem to indicate derision. For example, the word "pyramid" designated a cake of wheat and honey; an "obelisk" was a spit for roasting. These words were transmitted to the Western world, which retained them even after the Egyptian language was deciphered and the original terms were identified.

The word sphinx was also retained, but why was it chosen to designate the reality of a sphinx? The question remains open. The term scarcely occurs in what the Greek historians wrote about Giza, for the simple reason that the Sphinx was largely unknown to them. It is not until the Roman writer Pliny that we hear of it under this name, which passed into Latin. But in another context, Herodotus (*Histories*, II, 175), listing the works of Amasis at Sais, mentions "androsphinxes," which Hellenists hesitatingly interpret as "male sphinxes" or "man-headed sphinxes." Much later, in Apollodorus, the word sphinx designated a symbolic representation of the sun, evoking certain aspects of the theology of Harmakhis, whom the Greeks regarded as a form of their sun god Helios. But in the fifth century B.C.E., when Herodotus visited Egypt, he saw sphinxes, including the one at Giza, though he did not mention it. Did the Greeks associate these sphinxes with the cruel figure defeated by Oedipus? The physical resemblance is rather distant, except for some representations of female winged sphinxes. All in all, the combination of an animal body and a human head was perhaps sufficient to choose this appellation. But it seems rather forced to compare the solar character of Harmakhis in the New Kingdom, with his triple form of Khepri—the sun rising in the morning, Re at noon, and Atum, the sun setting in the evening—to Oedipus' response to the riddle of the sphinx regarding the infant, the adult, and the old man. Some have not hesitated to do so,[2] but other considerations rebut the comparison. In the first place, the

[2] Selim Hassan, *The Great Sphinx of Giza* (Cairo, 1953), 209–11. This interpretation has often been repeated in psychoanalytic literature, though it is feebly supported by the evidence.

analogy is valid only for Harmakhis, and not for sphinxes in general. Further, the Greek historians never mention the Sphinx of Giza. It seems doubtful that they had the means of knowing this theological particular, which is clearly expressed only in the text of the stela of Tuthmosis IV. Otherwise, the Greeks always distinguished between male and female sphinxes. A Hellenistic fresco discovered at Tuna el-Gebel represents Oedipus before a sphinx in the traditional Greek manner. Finally, a decree from the second century C.E., written in Greek, salutes the Sphinx of Giza as a beneficent deity, contrasting it with the beast of Boeotian Thebes.

This term sphinx has prompted other questions and other equally doubtful comparisons. Although the Greeks drew on their own vocabulary to name Egyptian realities unfamiliar to them, some scholars have taken the opposite tack and have searched for an Egyptian word that could have been transformed into "sphinx." They have proposed that the Egyptian term *shesep-ankh* was the origin of the word "sphinx," though this is scarcely imaginable from a phonetic point of view. They have developed another, parallel argument that begins with the Egyptian language. *Shesep-ankh* designates a statue—a "living image," as the Egyptians called it—and it is an item in the rich vocabulary designating representations that could be outlined in two dimensions or realized in the form of a statue. In some cases, the word is determined by the image of a sphinx.[3] It takes only a single step to make *shesep-ankh* the term for sphinx in the Egyptian language. Yet a systematic study of the occurrences of this expression shows that its use is not restricted to depictions of sphinxes, but rather that it is applied to statues of all sorts. Viewing it as the specific term for a sphinx is thus incorrect. In certain contexts, it can allude to such statues, but it is not confined to them. The name Haremakhet, moreover, was not a designation of sphinxes, but was applied only to the Sphinx of Giza, and only from the New Kingdom on. This absence of a distinct term should not surprise us. The idea of the sphinx was that of a royal statue, which could be given an appropriate designation but not a specific one; taxonomy differs from one language to another. When the Sphinx of Giza received a new interpretation, it was given a specific and appropriate name that was not a generic designation.

[3] A determinative, or semiogram, is a sign that in principle ends a word. The determinative is not read out loud; rather, it indicates the category to which an object belongs, or a type of activity if it is a matter of an abstract term.

2

The Modern History of the Sphinx

To know an archaeological monument, to arrive at the state of knowledge that we can present at this time, we must trace the history of excavations and analyze their results, something that was not necessarily done by the excavators themselves. Future work, of course, might nullify some of our conclusions or force us to refine others.

The earliest archaeologists often made major discoveries; after all, they were likely to work on "virgin soil," sites in the condition in which they had been abandoned at the end of antiquity. These digs are an essential part of our information, for they present an area and its monuments in essentially the final state in which they were utilized by the ancient Egyptians. Yet these adventurous pioneers left only brief notes—if any—regarding their finds and the course of their excavations. This point is not made to cast aspersions at these early excavators, for their working conditions were more difficult than those of a contemporary archaeologist. The attitude toward antiquities was also not the same. Excavations began at some sites even before the decipherment of the hieroglyphs, which prevented a reading of the texts and led to interpretations that today are viewed as totally erroneous. Moreover, archaeology long remained a hunt for objects, the contexts of which scarcely mattered. What was true for the first half of the nineteenth century remained largely so for nearly another hundred years.

Important digs have regularly been undertaken in the area of the Sphinx from the early nineteenth century to the present. Even the work that yielded the most results, such as that of Émile Baraize from 1920 to 1930 and the campaigns of Selim Hassan from 1936 to 1938, remains poorly documented; in the absence of detailed plans, determining where an object was discovered is impossible. Nevertheless, it is from these results, complemented by contemporary excavations, that we must attempt to write a history of the Sphinx. This is all the more so given that these brief excavation reports, these few drawings, or later, photographs, are the only evidence of levels that have disappeared in the meanwhile. Archaeology unavoidably has two sides. Uncovering buried material and thus enabling the recovery of cross sections of the past entails the inexorable destruction of strata, representing levels of occupation, that were sometimes superimposed on one another during more than two millennia. There is no other way to reach the lower levels, the most ancient ones, than to remove irretrievably, one at a time, the more recent ones. After that, only the records—the drawings, notes, and photographs—inform us of them. In the matter of discovered objects, the situation is somewhat different. If they are in a museum or a local storehouse, it is still possible to study them, to reinterpret them, and to integrate them into a larger corpus, even when their archaeological context remains imprecise. It is by means of this double approach, accompanied by a review of the archaeological work, that we have enough material to tackle a site or a particular monument such as the Sphinx.

FROM ANTIQUITY TO THE TWENTIETH CENTURY

Numerous sources prove that in the Greco-Roman Period, access to the Sphinx was carefully preserved, and that it continued to be worshiped, whether by natives or by Greeks. Herodotus (*Histories*, II, 124–35) offers the first "historical" witness of a foreigner writing about Egypt, which he visited during the first Persian domination; he devotes pages to the Giza plateau and its pyramids, mixing historically verifiable elements with others that belong to legend. But he makes no mention of the Sphinx, which is astonishing, for at that time, the *temenos*[1] of the statue was cleared and in

---

[1] A sacred space, separated from profane space by an enclosure wall.

use, its cult attested. This same silence is found in his successors, Diodorus Siculus and Strabo, and in Manetho, an Egyptian historian who wrote in Greek; these writers often borrowed information from their predecessors, which could explain this persistent absence. Only Pliny in his *Natural History*, written in the first century of our own era, mentions the Sphinx and the tourist-related activities of the residents of the nearby village, the Letopolite Busiris; quite like the dragomen of the nineteenth century, these villagers would climb to the summit of Cheops' pyramid. Unfortunately, the contemporaries of this activity-filled site did not leave detailed information concerning what they saw and heard.

When the pagan cults were closed by decree of the emperor Theodosius in the fourth century C.E., the site of Giza gradually fell victim to the invading sands. Egypt became Christian, and centuries later, there was the Arab conquest and the Islamization of the land. The site of the Great Pyramids and the Sphinx, on the edge of the eastern desert at the apex of Cairo, was not a propitious location for urban settlement, nor had it been during the pharaonic era, when Memphis, some twenty miles south of Cairo, had played the role of great metropolis of the north. It is hardly surprising that few traces of the Coptic (i.e., Christian) era have been found in the neighborhood, unlike the situation at sites that were constantly occupied and in which pharaonic ruins were transformed into churches or monasteries. Yet this realization offers a bit of satisfaction to the Egyptologist: an assurance that this abandoned site, buried under the sand, remained untouched until excavations were first undertaken. This was true for the Sphinx, but the accounts of Western travelers reveal a different state of affairs for the pyramids. During the Middle Ages, these monuments served as quarries for the construction of buildings in Cairo, like many other Egyptian sites that were unhesitatingly stripped of their stone by medieval builders.

Though they rarely alluded to this fact, Arab historians, geographers, and travelers in no way ignored the Great Pyramids and the Sphinx. Many of them mentioned the site; and while their descriptions are not very instructive, they reveal many legends that were embellished between the eleventh and the eighteenth centuries, when a new era was inaugurated by Napoleon's expedition to Egypt. Arab scholars who mentioned the Sphinx include the geographer Maqrizi, in his *Topographical and Historical*

Description of Egypt; Abd el-Latif Bagdadi; and Murtada ibn al Afif. All described the head that alone emerged from the sand southeast of the pyramid of Chephren. The past was a closed book, and the pyramids were attributed to new owners, the most famous of whom was Surid. The Sphinx head, which was understood to rest on a body that was entirely buried, received the name Balhouba in Coptic; in Arabic, this became Abu'l Hol, "Father of Terror," a designation it bears to this day. A taxi driver in Cairo knows where to take you if you ask for the Sphinx, but when speaking with the workers on a dig, you always hear the words Abu'l Hol. The strange sight of a head emerging from the sand could not have failed to inspire fear, especially given that all sorts of maleficent genies and ghouls were said to roam the neighborhood. Yet other texts report that this bodiless head, far from being maleficent, was regarded as a talisman that protected the surrounding area, especially the crops, a role that is found in Greek texts inscribed on votive objects.

Another bit of folklore concerns the Sphinx's face. Its human face is relatively well preserved, unlike the lion's body, but the nose is missing. Guides claim that this damage is the result of cannon fire from Napoleon's soldiers, undoubtedly the guides' way of noting their disapproval of his expedition to Egypt. Today, the damage is often attributed to the vengefulness of the Mamelukes, who ruled Egypt in the fourteenth century. But from the tenth century on, Arab writers reported that the damage was a result of iconoclastic zeal. Finally, the recent study by archaeologist Mark Lehner shows clear traces of destruction by tools of an indeterminate era that must therefore be situated between the third and the tenth centuries. We must also cite a delightful work, the *Book of Buried Pearls and Precious Mysteries: On the Indications of Cachettes, Finds, and Treasures,* a fantasy-filled manual that, as its title indicates, was intended to facilitate the discovery of fabulous and mythic treasures left behind by the ancient Egyptians. The area around the Great Pyramids and the Sphinx aroused the greed of those who read the book, who scarcely differed in this respect from our own contemporaries who hunt for Cathar treasure and the like.

Along with the texts of the Eastern writers were many accounts by pilgrims en route to the Holy Land; from the eleventh century on, they journeyed via Egypt, which in the seventeenth century became a travel destination in itself. The long list of travelers who recounted their visit to the site of Giza includes Benjamin of Tuleda, Prosper Alpin, Pierre Belon, Jean de Thévenot, Father Vansleb, Paul Lucas, and, in the eighteenth century, Frederick Norden and Karsten Niebuhr. Throughout the Middle Ages, a legend purported that the pyramids were the "Granaries of Joseph," which the latter supposedly constructed to provide for the years of famine predicted by his interpretation of Pharaoh's dream. But later travelers, thanks to their acquaintance with the Greek writers, realized that these were the tombs of Cheops, Chephren, and Mycerinus, and they also mentioned the head of the Sphinx. Some of them claimed that the Sphinx was linked to the tomb of Cheops by a tunnel. Among these accounts, that of Father Vansleb evokes the atmosphere and the spirit of the age. Norden's engravings, and others as well, convey what these travelers saw: the Sphinx buried in sand in front of the pyramids of Cheops and Chephren, the latter a bit too steep, as they were depicted in those days. Some of the accounts are more baroque, such as the view by Olfert Dapper in his *Naukeurige beschrijvinge der Afrikaensche gewesten van Egypten, Barbaryen, Libyen* (Precise description of the African regions of Egypt, Barbary, Libya), which was published in Amsterdam in 1668. Long before the scholars of Bonaparte's expedition prepared the famous plate depicting the Grand Gallery of the pyramid of Cheops, their predecessors had already visited this pyramid, penetrating this long corridor all the way to the King's Chamber. But no one attempted to clear the Sphinx; though it aroused great wonder, the hour of discovery was yet to come.

THE ERA OF EXCAVATIONS

Though Napoleon's military operations in Egypt ended in fiasco, the tremendous results obtained in scarcely three years by the galaxy of scholars, artists, and specialists who accompanied his expedition aroused an intense fascination with Egypt. This passion not only caused a lasting interest in this land, which was led into a new era by Mohammed Aly; it also stimulated the work of pioneers of archaeology, even before Jean-François Champollion succeeded in deciphering the hieroglyphs in 1822. But at Giza, Napoleon's scholars undertook only limited work. Some plates and the accompanying text by Edmé Jomard summarize their activity: classic investigation of the pyramid of Cheops; exploration of the large, carefully planned cemeteries distributed over several areas of the plateau; and a superficial cleaning of the back of the Sphinx. That cleaning, however, did not enable a total clearing of the animal's body, despite the legend that sprang up half a century later: Auguste Mariette's workers claimed that Napoleon's scholars had found a door leading to the interior of the Sphinx. We are reminded of the stela of Tuthmosis IV located between the legs, but if it had been discovered at that time, we would at least have had an image of it in the plates of the *Description de l'Égypte*.

The first pioneers who attempted to clear the Sphinx needed a great deal of passion and perhaps a dose of foolhardiness; they risked not only their workers' lives but their own as well. In 1817, Giovanni Caviglia worked for the consul Henry Salt, a great collector, as many excavators were at that time. He began by digging a trench that enabled him to reach the northern shoulder of the Sphinx and to go down as far as the rock that constituted the floor of the sanctuary of the colossus. This was the first time since antiquity that part of the animal's body, covered by a casing of limestone blocks, had been brought to light again. The trench, which was sixty-five feet deep, was funnel-shaped, and although the sides were held in place by a system of planks, they continually threatened to collapse and to swallow up the workmen. The method was dangerous, yet Caviglia later resumed his work in front of the head of the Sphinx, this time arriving at the forelegs, which he cleared; between them, he discovered the pink granite stela of Tuthmosis IV, which remains in place to this day. It constituted the back wall of a small chapel between the front legs of the animal, against which leaned low walls bearing two stelae of Ramesses II. Among the various objects discovered were a cobra's head, from the uraeus that once adorned the forehead of the Sphinx, and a fragment of its plaited beard. These results, which were remarkable enough, inspired Caviglia to extend his investigations toward the east. He discovered the gigantic Roman Period installation that had given access to the sanctuary during the final era in which it had been in use. Two flights of stairs separated by a huge landing led down to the paving that covered the natural rock. Greek texts found in the area confirmed that this work was carried out in the first and second centuries of our own era. Only a few sketches permit us to imagine the appearance of this site when it was abandoned. They are all the more precious in that later excavations entailed the destruction of nearly all of this complex. A partial clearing without any means of protection could only result in the monument's being rapidly covered by the sands once again, so thoroughly that during his scientific expedition of 1842–43, Richard Lepsius had to clear the chapel between the legs once again, along with the stela of Tuthmosis IV, of which he published the first copy. Meanwhile, Champollion had definitively charted the course of Egyptology with his decipherment of the hieroglyphic writing system.

Auguste Mariette engaged in prodigious activity, clearing many sites in Egypt for the first time in the modern era. In 1853 and 1858 he turned to the Sphinx, encountering the same difficulties as his predecessors. He also discovered the valley temple of the Chephren complex. As for the colossus, he managed to clear it totally of its rubble, and, not far from its northern flank, he found fragments of a statue that he identified as Osirid. At several points in the area, there emerged the remains of ancient walls of unbaked bricks that had protected the Sphinx temenos from the sands that were always ready to engulf it.

Gaston Maspero, Mariette's successor as director of the recently-created Antiquities Service, resumed work in 1885–86. Aside from his interest in penetrating what he considered the "mysteries" of the Sphinx, a more prosaic goal motivated him: to offer those tourists, already numerous in Egypt, who did not venture beyond Cairo an added attraction at the feet of the pyramids. To complete his work, he started a public subscription, but it proved insufficient; nonetheless, he managed to clear once more what Caviglia and Mariette had already exhumed. But again we have only hasty notes and not a single detailed report on the excavations. Picture postcards from the turn of the twentieth century, when photography was becoming popular, permit us a glimpse of the site as it appeared at that time. The history of the excavations conducted during the nineteenth century reflects an often undervalued fact: in thirty or forty years, a partially cleared sector can be covered anew by shifting soil and wind-blown sand. The Sphinx's location in its rocky cavity at the foot of the causeway of Chephren is susceptible to this perpetual movement that led, during the nineteenth century, to a veritable labor of Sisyphus. During periods of abandonment, after the end of the Old Kingdom and when activity came to an end in the Roman Period, less time than we might have believed was needed for the statue to disappear under many feet of accumulated debris. And when the site was in use, protective measures had to be taken continuously to keep it free of sand, as attested by both ancient texts and archaeological remains.

THE GREAT EXCAVATIONS OF THE TWENTIETH CENTURY

Although this historical summary centers on the Sphinx, it must be placed within the much larger framework of which this colossal figure is an integral part: the site of Giza, with its three pyramid complexes and the cemeteries of royal officials that surrounded them. During the nineteenth century, various excavations were conducted there in a somewhat unsystematic manner. In 1902, the work was rationalized by dividing the area into large concessions—American, Austrian, German, Italian, and Egyptian—some of which continued to World War II and beyond. During this period, the ambitious project of a general clearing of the area of the Sphinx was again undertaken under the auspices of the Antiquities Service, with the work led by Émile Baraize and Pierre Lacau (1925–36), and then by Selim Hassan (1936–38) for Cairo University. This was the most intense and the most fruitful period of all the excavations conducted around the Sphinx, and the perimeter was much wider than before. Well to the east, underneath the Roman levels known since the nineteenth century, excavations revealed a temple near the valley temple of Chephren, just north of the latter. Northeast of the Sphinx, Hassan discovered a chapel dedicated to Harmakhis by Amenophis II. In addition, many parts of the statue, which was in bad condition, were repaired. Thanks to the raising of a pile of rubble north of the Sphinx, the latter would from then on be in less danger of being once again engulfed by sand. Finally, while some structures were unfortunately destroyed, a large and varied mass of evidence was recovered: architectural elements, stelae, and votive objects made it possible to reconstruct the previously little-known history of Giza during the New Kingdom and the Late Period. Details of Baraize's excavations were never published, but his archives—notes, sketches, and in particular an invaluable collection of nearly three hundred photographs, most of them dated—make it possible to trace a good part of the work. A minute and perceptive analysis was carried out by

Mark Lehner beginning in 1979; he then drew on his investigations to prepare the first systematic archaeological description of the colossus. Hassan was more willing to publish than his predecessors. On many points—archaeological imprecision, lack of rigor in the presentation of objects, the translation and interpretation of texts—it is not always easy to profit from his publications; but at least they have made it possible for me to undertake a complete study of the material having to do with the Sphinx.

Subsequently, various excavations were conducted by the Antiquities Service in the vicinity of the colossus, and since 1979, important efforts have been made to restore the statue under the supervision of Zahi Hawass. The fall of a block drew numerous expert opinions, often contradictory, regarding the condition of the monument, which is threatened by the rise in the water table, as well as by aeolian erosion and ambient pollution. Proposals for salvage work sometimes bordered on the absurd, such as the gigantic bubble suggested by the Getty Foundation. Meanwhile, under the auspices of the American Research Center in Cairo, Lehner followed his annual campaigns with a detailed summary of his results, complete with photogrammetry and, for the first time, a plan of the Sphinx and its temenos.

Today, after nearly two centuries of excavations, we have attained a relatively satisfying degree of knowledge of the Sphinx. Nothing prevents our hoping for new discoveries, but they would undoubtedly bring nuances rather than an entirely different interpretation from that which can be proposed at the present time. Granted, a certain amount of evidence has been lost, and in this regard, with all scientific rigor, only hypotheses can be advanced. Despite the collecting of all possible information, our understanding of the period in which the project of the Sphinx was conceived and carried out remains highly limited. The reason is simple: in the earlier periods of their history, Egyptians left almost no written records regarding their religious beliefs. Intellectual rigor must therefore ally itself with caution; otherwise, we would descend into gratuitous and unverifiable assertions.

To someone who does not work daily with the evidence accumulated during nearly two centuries of Egyptology and who does not face the day-to-day difficulties of an excavation, it can seem surprising or even shocking that an especially prestigious monument could remain so poorly known for so long. Retracing the road that has been traveled has been useful, to show what problems had to be solved and to indicate how methods and perspectives have evolved. Doing so helps us to attain the goal that scholars set for themselves today: an analysis that takes account of all existing elements so as to arrive at an interpretation that is as free as possible from preconceived notions. The history of earlier excavations is not a matter of anecdotes; it is a fundamental part of our knowledge of a site that has experienced more change since the beginning of the nineteenth century than it did from the end of antiquity to the outset of archaeological investigations.

3

Description and History of the Sphinx

Though the Great Sphinx is recognized by all, until recently, it has been one of the least known and least studied monuments from a strictly archaeological point of view. Despite its deteriorated condition, visitors, whether tourists or Egyptologists, have always been struck by the grandeur, the strength, and the tranquillity emanating from this colossus, with the gigantic mass of the pyramids serving as its backdrop. From simply being awed by the monument's grandeur to making an architectural study was a big step that was a long time in coming, however. The archaeologists of the nineteenth century left only brief reports or none at all. Their primary goal was to clear the monument from the sands. Specialists in the pyramids, such as Jean-Philippe Lauer, I. E. S. Edwards, or more recently, Rainer Stadelmann, who have written books about these royal tombs, have of course included the Sphinx in their descriptions of Giza; but their discussions are brief, giving its basic measurements, noting its location in the Chephren complex, and mentioning documents relating to it, notably the stela of Tuthmosis IV. Again, these are only brief surveys.

We must also note a few studies that deal with the age of the Sphinx. Even in the land where the colossal was a part of the landscape, this statue is of an unusual size, the largest of all those known from Egypt. Since it bears no inscription permitting a straightforward and certain dating, hypotheses abound, some of them far-fetched and based on not a single valid argu-

ment. For some authors, the Sphinx can date back only to an extremely remote age, long before Dynasty 4, with no further specification. For these
authors, such speculation is clearly a matter of vague sentiment with nothing to support it. For others, including Mariette and Maspero—at least in
some of their works—the Sphinx does not date to a protohistorical period,
but in any event it predates the reign of Cheops. Their conclusion resulted
from a literal, but erroneous, reading of the Stela of the Daughter of
Cheops, which was soon called into question. Others, including Ludwig
Borchardt and Georges Daressy, based their estimates on unreliable stylistic
comparisons and concluded that the Sphinx was a work of the Middle
Kingdom, carved when the site lay abandoned and already invaded by sand.
Again, the sloppy reasoning is easy to refute. All these scholars lacked sufficient material for comparison; we have few sphinxes from the Old Kingdom, which led them to make the colossus a witness to a much earlier period—or, the opposite, to date it to the Middle Kingdom. As
comprehensive study of Giza progressed, scholars soon realized that the
Sphinx was part of the funerary complex of Chephren and that its face was
sculpted in the image of this pharaoh. We now have more than two hundred
statues or statue fragments of various sizes from this king's funerary and valley temples; no equivalent phenomenon exists in any other mortuary complex. Not until the 1980s did an archaeologist set out to analyze the Great
Sphinx from the point of view of any Egyptian monument with a history
that stretched from the beginning of the second millennium B.C.E. to the
Roman Period. To accomplish this, in addition to studying unpublished
archival material, Mark Lehner conducted many seasons of survey and excavation that finally led to a detailed and faithful study of the statue. His
work shed light on its changes and especially on the succession of phases of
destruction and restoration, though some of them remain unknown. These
results, combined with research on all the material found in the area of the
Sphinx and a critical reading of the texts dedicated to it in the New Kingdom, the Late Period, and the Greco-Roman Period, enabled him to reconstruct much of a history that had remained obscure until then.

An architectural description of the monument was the necessary pre-
liminary to a study of the religious evolution of this figure, which was
royal at first, and secondarily divine. The architectural results were arrived
at with the help of geological research carried out on the plateau; this re-

search helped establish the particulars of the erosion of the animal's body. These investigations also revealed the phases of work on Chephren's funerary complex—the time when the quarries began to be worked, and the use of their stone for the construction of individual monuments—thus enabling a definitive reconstruction of their chronological order on the basis of the materials employed.

The entire Sphinx was constructed in the body of the rocky plateau that rises above the alluvial plain and served as the quarry for the monuments that were erected on the plateau. Granite was transported downriver from the Aswan region, while the casing stones of fine white limestone came from the area of Tura on the opposite bank of the Nile. Because of its geological history, the rock of the western desert, which is usually called nummulitic limestone, is heterogeneous, consisting of successive layers of widely differing quality; the layers offer unequal resistance to erosion, which is mostly aeolian but is also caused by sand. This explains the uneven degradation of the body of the Sphinx, which has flaked away to a greater or lesser degree from one layer to the next. This phenomenon was recognized by the Egyptians, who took it into account when they skillfully laid out the complex.

The Sphinx is located at the lower edge of the plateau that constitutes the platform of the three Great Pyramids, north of the causeway of Chephren and west of the so-called Sphinx temple. This area is composed of a series of terraces that are somewhat unequal in height. The valley temple of Chephren is in the lowest part, and from there, the causeway leads up to the funerary temple; the facades of the valley temple and the Sphinx temple are almost exactly aligned. The temenos of the Sphinx—in other words, the quarry from which it emerges—is nearly 330 feet long and 200 feet wide; it is on a slightly higher level than the two temples, and it is dominated on the north by the area that abuts on the southern edge of the eastern cemetery of Cheops. The southern boundary of the temenos is cut into the rock parallel to the causeway of Chephren, while its western edge separates it from an overhanging sector that long remained unoccupied, until the Saite Period.

The cavity around the Sphinx has the shape of a U facing east, the direction in which the statue is turned. The Sphinx is not aligned with the axis of the Dynasty 4 temple in front of it, nor does it have direct communication with this temple. It was long believed that the Sphinx was conceived and realized on the basis of a core of rock that remained in a quarry opened during the reign of Cheops to furnish blocks for the construction of his pyramid. This interpretation assigns a large role to chance, maintaining that the very idea of this colossal sphinx was dictated by the chance circumstances of the site. The shape of a spur of rock left behind in a quarry supposedly inspired a plan to sculpt it into the form of a lion with a human head. Such a proposition poses many questions to which there are no satisfying responses. If such was the case, why did Chephren rather than Cheops decide the fate of this unshaped outcrop of rock? Further, it is atypical of the Egyptian way of thinking to use a remnant of rock to give it a particular shape, in this case that of a sphinx, of which it is almost certainly the prototype. Everything in the layout of the Giza plateau suggests planning that was not subject to accidents in the terrain. If these considerations are not sufficient, there is one that cannot be called into question. The quarry of the Sphinx was not exploited by Cheops, but by Chephren. The slopes of the layers of limestone, which are perfectly visible on the southern wall of the temenos, are also found on the blocks constituting the basic material of the Sphinx temple, which must have been covered with stone of better quality. This building, entirely without inscriptions, is close to the valley temple of Chephren and is quite similar to the latter in its construction; it can date only to the reign of Chephren, thus dating the use of the quarry that was transformed into a sanctuary for the Sphinx. The colossal statue was sculpted in the reign of that pharaoh, as an integral part of his complex, which is a unique instance, not only at Giza, but also in all the royal funerary complexes.

Geological analysis of the terrain confirms what is visible to the naked eye. The floor of the Sphinx depression, which was leveled in its entirety, constitutes a solid level of rock that has stood up to the vicissitudes of weather, and which also forms the lower part of the animal's body. Above this lower part, the body of the lion, up to its neck, was carved in an extremely heterogeneous area of rock with friable layers. The layers are rich in clay and have suffered considerable disintegration, giving the cross section its characteristic appearance of a series of concave and convex surfaces. But the head—and this can scarcely be the result of chance—was sculpted in a much harder layer of rock that better endured the effects of erosion, though it has also experienced the ravages of time. There is reason to think that the dimensions of the colossus were calculated in terms of this upper layer of stone out of which its head was carved.

The length of the animal totals 238 feet; its height is just over 65 feet, and that of its back is 40 feet. These dimensions make it the largest known colossus, with the peculiarity that it is physically a part of the plateau itself, though the Sphinx was later treated as if it were a statue.[1] At least in its present condition, only the head has the appearance of a finished sculpture whose elements are entirely visible. With its *nemes* (Figure 3), the head is practically cube-shaped, the face corresponding to a square of about 33 feet on each side. Its eyes, somewhat deep-set under brows carved in relief, and its tightly pursed lips have suffered somewhat from damage. Its nose, which has entirely disappeared, cannot be restored (Figure 4). Notwithstanding its size, the sculptor was able to endow this head with a solemn serenity that renders it less severe than the famous head of Chephren in the Cairo Museum. Neither the changes wrought by time nor human attacks have robbed it of its beauty, which remains striking. The Sphinx still bears traces of red paint, which might have been added after the Old Kingdom. Leaving the ears free (Figure 5) and falling back in two broad, triangular sections, the *nemes* is covered with relief-carved stripes that have eroded in the back. The ends of these sections, which once rested on the shoulders, disappeared long ago, adding to the fragility of the badly eroded neck. Here and there on the statue, Baraize effected restorations using limestone blocks that partially replaced these missing parts. The top of the head is quite flat and is provided with a hole. A uraeus, the upper part of which is broken off, is attached to the top of the forehead. Part of a cobra was recovered during Caviglia's excavations, but no one has been able to determine whether this fragment is original or whether it stems from a later restoration. The back of the *nemes*, which usually consists of a knot and a piece of cloth, is also missing. The poor condition of the back of the head, as well as that of the top of the Sphinx's back, does not allow for restoration, however, nor can we know whether

[1] Only in the Ramesside Period do we find colossal statues that can be compared, *mutatis mutandis*, with the Sphinx. Those of Ramesses II in front of the great temple at Abu Simbel, which were also carved directly into the rock, reach a height of about 66 feet.

Figure 3. Head and torso of the Sphinx during the repairs of 1925. Archives Lacau. Centre W. Golenischeff, EPHE, Vᵉ section.

Figure 4. Detail of the face of the Sphinx: the right eye and the broken nose, 1926.
Archives Lacau. Centre W. Golenischeff, EPHE,Vᵉ section.

Figure 5. Detail of the right ear and the *nemes* of the Sphinx, 1926. Archives Lacau. Centre W. Golenischeff, EPHE, V^e section.

repairs were made on this part of the statue at some indeterminate time in the past. Taking scale into account, a comparison of the entire head and the *nemes* with that of a statue of Chephren seems to offer a correspondence.

A final unresolved question regarding the face concerns the beard. Today the Sphinx is beardless, but numerous representations from the New Kingdom depict it with a long false beard, plaited and curved, a divine prerogative distinct from the short, squared beard worn by kings and royal sphinxes. Once again, the early excavations prove valuable. Caviglia discovered many pieces belonging to the beard and the tenon that joined it to the breast. The quality of the limestone appears to be the same as that of the body of the animal. Was this beard, which was nearly 30 feet long, conceived from the very beginning? It clearly experienced repair, if not a complete restoration, at the time of the New Kingdom. The tenon would have rested on the protuberance at the lower third of the breast. This type of beard seems highly unusual for the Old Kingdom, though there are a few parallels with which it can be compared.

The protuberance itself (Figure 6) also has raised questions. It seems never to have been covered with a limestone casing, as were the legs and the flanks of the animal. It supposedly existed already in Dynasty 4, and there must have been a reason for its existence. Some scholars have regarded this now-unshaped mass as the remnant of a statue that would have been sculpted in the rock that constitutes the Sphinx. It is possible to find parallels, but nothing permits us to suggest a date for such a sculpture, the Old Kingdom being excluded. On the basis of his archaeological analysis, Lehner felt he could demonstrate that a separate royal colossus had been placed just below the beard, against this protuberance, while its base was level with the top of the stela of Tuthmosis IV. The hypothesis is plausible, because of traces on the chest, but we have no proof of the existence of a separate colossus, which supposedly would have dated back to Dynasty 18. There remains the question of the appearance of this part of the body before the statue was associated with it, if that was indeed what happened.

The forelegs of the Sphinx, which are extensions of the body, stretch out parallel to each other. Their outsize length has long been noted and attributed to the successive repairs of the rock core, which was covered

Figure 6. The Sphinx, with its head encased in scaffolding, 1925. The protuberance on the chest is particularly visible here. Archives Lacau. Centre W. Golenischeff, EPHE, V^e section.

with a casing of limestone blocks during various stages of its history; the modern repairs include work by Baraise. The repairs of the Roman Period can be distinguished from the Greek dedications and prayers to Harmakhis inscribed on these blocks. In fact, a systematic cleaning has shown that the thickness of the casing is slight compared with the original size of the legs, which in no way explains their unusual length. The latter should in fact be connected with the total length of the animal. If we make a scale comparison between a sphinx sculptured in the round in classical statuary and the Sphinx of Giza, we see that the Sphinx, when viewed from the side, is poorly proportioned, with too small a head compared with the length of the body and the legs. This phenomenon was likely not the result of clumsiness on the part of the stonemasons, but rather was caused by geological difficulties they encountered: deep faults in the body of the animal required giving it a large size to assure that it would remain intact.

As can be seen today where the rock is bare, the body is badly eroded, with convex indentations due to the wearing away of the more friable layers. The rear legs are tucked under the flanks. The tail lies along the right haunch. The top of the back is quite flat, with cracks and a cavity, explored long ago by Mariette; though the cavity was long taken to be a burial pit, it is only a natural hollow. Part of the limestone casing is still in place. Several factors indicate three distinct phases, not counting modern repairs. The size of the blocks, the quality of their stone, the mortar between the blocks, and the traces of tools all differ according to period. In the first two phases, the same type of Tura limestone was employed, but the other criteria are quite distinct. In the final phase, a more friable stone was employed. The first period of restoration, which undoubtedly saw work on the entire body, likely dates back to the New Kingdom, and probably to Tuthmosis IV, who also had a stela set up between the forelegs (Figure 7). All this work was carried out using materials from the site itself. The stela matches the back of a door lintel undoubtedly stemming from Chephren's funerary temple, while the casing stones were cut from Tura limestone taken from earlier monuments, such as the nearby causeway of Chephren. This reuse of the site as a quarry while the cemetery was still in use should not surprise us. The Egyptians employed this practice throughout their history, without viewing it as a sign of desecration, and the practice enabled them to construct and to embellish new installations that suited the needs of the moment at less expense. The second stage marks the restoration of the earlier casing, which had eroded over the centuries. Certain indications link this work to other works that were carried out in Dynasty 26. This restoration took place during a historical period that saw intense activity on the Giza plateau. Finally, the Sphinx was renewed in the era of Roman domination, as specified clearly in the texts of certain decrees, and a huge esplanade with a staircase leading to the monument was constructed. Analysis of the casing blocks has facilitated a relatively precise dating of the stages of work carried out on the statue. During a long period beginning with the New Kingdom, the Sphinx seemed to be a man-made object. The rock core that composed the bulk of its volume was entirely covered, and perhaps painted, which made it possible to hide the somewhat disastrous effects of erosion. The initial stage of restoration followed a period of wear, as shown by archaeological investigation: the blocks that were used were fitted into convex

Figure 7. The stela of Tuthmosis IV between the forelegs of the Sphinx. Archives
Golenischeff. Centre W. Golenischeff, EPHE, V^e section.

spaces that had been hollowed out, so as to fill them. Four limestone constructions were added to the north and south flanks of the animal; they
resemble bases with tops closed by slabs, and they belong for the most part
to the first stage of restoration in the New Kingdom. According to Mariette, the largest one, on the north, served as the base of an Osirid statue, a
hypothesis later repeated at length by Lehner.[2] These additional constructions in fact remain rather mysterious.

Other questions concern the original appearance of the colossus when
it was carved during Dynasty 4, for only the face has not been retouched.
Did it originally have a casing? Had one been intended but not added?
Or was there merely a sort of filler to hide the irregularities in the rock?
In a few of the denuded portions of the monument, indications have been
found of an attempt at finishing touches, such as the traces of a nail on
one of the toes, but the surface was never polished in its entirety. The
question of finishing touches during the Old Kingdom remains, and undoubtedly will continue to remain, without an answer. If erosion could
have the devastating effects we have observed, perhaps we should think
that in Dynasty 4, the body received no protection and that its deteriora-
tion began then, before it was entirely covered by sand, and that the sand
offered no protection but rather acted as an eroding agent. The end of the
Roman Empire also could have been devastating to the Sphinx; at that
time the monument was no longer maintained and was gradually covered
with sand again.

Thus, a long history has influenced the monument's present appearance, which continued to change during the 1980s and 1990s with the
work carried out by the Egyptian Antiquities Organization.[3] This history
leads us from the choice made by Chephren's architects to fashion a
colossal sphinx, an audacious work, in a quarry laid out for that purpose,
down to the final undertakings of the Roman prefects of Egypt, by way of
creating a limestone casing, in the New Kingdom, which was repaired in
the Saite Period.

---

[2] See chapter 5, where I critique the interpretation and restoration proposed by Lehner.

[3] The Sphinx has experienced other vicissitudes linked to contemporary historical
events. During World War II, when it was feared that German forces would bombard Cairo,
a gigantic protective wall of stone was built from the ground up to the chin of the statue,
hiding its chest. The wall was not dismantled until the 1950s.

4

The Old Kingdom: The Sphinx as Part of the Chephren Funerary Complex

Since the Sphinx was not an isolated element on the Giza plateau, but rather part of a funerary complex, we must attempt to understand the goal that motivated the sculpting of this colossal figure in a quarry at the lower edge of the plateau. For the scholar who values objectivity, this goal is the trickiest aspect of the Sphinx to consider, for no contemporary text explains the role of each element in the funerary layout, or of this unparalleled statue in particular. We too often think of Egypt as the land of writing *par excellence*, but to do so is to forget that during the early centuries of Egyptian history, the most famous monuments, such as the Great Pyramids of Giza and their funerary temples, were not inscribed. In addition, although the walls of the mastabas (rectangular tomb structures) surrounding the pyramids bear inscriptions that enable us to identify their owners and their families and to acquaint ourselves with the details of daily life, we know little about the history of the sovereigns of Dynasty 4 and about their religious thought. Even though we can draw somewhat on texts carved on the interior walls of pyramids of Dynasties 5 and 6, these texts are difficult to interpret, and they do not answer all the questions we ask when faced with the silent constructions of the Giza plateau. This lack of documents should admonish us to remain cautious and modest. If one wishes to construct hypotheses—and that is scarcely difficult to do—one should at least adhere to this rule and not slip from conjecture to simple affirmations based on no demonstrable proof. Yet that is what often happens. The Sphinx, in particular, has inspired interpretations that are not tenable for Dynasty 4.

Today, most Egyptologists agree that the Sphinx was an integral part of the funerary complex of Chephren, whom it depicts in the form of a lion with a human head. Some, however, have attributed the Sphinx to the reign of Cheops. Granted, the Sphinx is situated north of Chephren's causeway, but this does not justify including it in the domain of Cheops, to which nothing attaches it from the point of view of general topography or architectural concept. Yet recognizing the Sphinx as the image of Chephren is not enough; it is also necessary to understand, if possible, the *raison d'être* and the meaning of the statue. A widely accepted idea, proposed by Selim Hassan and followed by others, views the Sphinx as guardian of the funerary complex of Chephren and of the cemetery as a whole. This is a vague claim that rests on debatable associations. Sphinxes, which are depictions of kings, do not in fact have a protective function. Hassan therefore had to cite much later religious texts that represent two lions, back to back, sometimes replaced by sphinxes; these lions were guardians of the netherworld, and the sun is depicted rising between them as though emerging from the horizon. But such representations are far removed from the Sphinx of Giza, and no evidence compels us to make this connection. The Sphinx has also been interpreted as a form of Horus, and this is a trickier question. If the statue is supposed to be a representation of Horus the sky god, the suggestion carries no force of conviction, for this was not his usual image, especially in this very early period. In addition, statues of deities are rare from this period, though some dyads and triads depict Mycerinus accompanied by one or two divine figures. We would be more justified in referring to the king in his name and aspect of Horus; this god was already a part of his titulary (the king's group of titles and names) in the Old Kingdom. The divine guise of the king, Horus on earth, would be incarnate in this statue. In any event, this explanation seems plausible—and the least hazardous, for it introduces no serious anachronism into our picture of the religious history of Giza in the Old Kingdom.

At this point, another problem intervenes. When Auguste Mariette discovered Chephren's valley temple in the 1850s, he called it the temple of the Sphinx because of its proximity to the statue; he cleared the temple and found statues of the king in it. In the early twentieth century, Uvo Hölscher resumed excavations and published the monument; since then, we have been able to explain its purpose. The temple served to receive the corpse of the deceased king, and funerary rites were performed on the body in the temple before the body was taken to the funerary temple on the eastern face of the pyramid. Later, Émile Baraize and then Hassan partially cleared another temple just north of the valley temple; it had been unknown until then, for it was buried under debris, piled higher than its roof, that had served as the foundation for later constructions. It was only in 1965–67 that the excavations were completed and the monument published. From then on this was called the temple of the Sphinx, because it is situated just in front of the latter. Built in alignment with the valley temple, it is later than that temple and later than the Sphinx. Nevertheless, it was erected during the reign of Chephren. While its plan differs substantially from that of the valley temple, it also displays analogies to the latter with respect to architectural technique. Despite its poor state of preservation, its excavator, Herbert Ricke, was able to show that its exterior remained unfinished and that the blocks of local limestone had never received a granite casing. But such a casing was attached to the interior, and its floor was paved with alabaster. The plan of this interior experienced changes during the building's construction. The temple, which is oriented east-west, was entered through two doors that gave access, via two corridors with niches, to an open-air court. The latter is surrounded by pillars against which colossal statues apparently rested, to judge from the size of the bases. All around this court, a second colonnade of twenty-four monolithic granite pillars was set in place in two phases, with each side comprising six pillars. To the east and to the west, two additional pillars flank a niche. The northern part of the court supposedly included an altar intended for offerings, with a drain for the flow of liquids. Such is the quick description we can make of this monument, which was published with great archaeological precision but with a number of fragile hypotheses.

Questions also arise about interpreting a monument that bears no inscriptions, thus opening the way to daring speculations. Still, some points can be established as certain. The Sphinx temple is the most ancient temple known that did not serve a funerary purpose. In fact, the king's mortuary complex was complete with its valley temple—which must have had a quay in front of it for the docking of boats—along with its sloping causeway, its actual funerary temple, and the pyramid serving as a tomb. The edifice situated just in front of the Sphinx is not oriented along the same axis as the statue. There is a discrepancy of more than seven yards; the axis of the Sphinx, which is also east-west, passes through the location of the presumed altar in the northern part of the temple. Finally, there is no direct access from the building to the depression of the Sphinx, which in Dynasty 4 could have been reached only by skirting the southern or the northern end of the temple, where there were two open-air corridors. The southern corridor separated the valley temple from the temple of the Sphinx, while the northern corridor is bounded on one side by the edifice and on the other side by the rock itself, which was cut back to accommodate it. Given the proximity of the statue and the temple—it seems difficult not to see a relationship between them—this lack of direct access between the two monuments seems strange. What link could have existed between the two?

The features of the building, with its large open-air court surrounded by a double colonnade, remind us of a temple intended for a solar cult, like those built later at Abu-Ghurab and Abusir by the monarchs of Dynasty 5. The excavators, Herbert Ricke and Siegfried Schott, wished to go much further in their interpretation. The twelve colossal statues that would have been set up in the court supposedly represented the twelve months of the year, while the twenty-four pillars of the outer colonnade stood for the twelve hours of the day and the twelve hours of the night. Further, the additional pillars to the east and the west would be the stylized arms and legs of the goddess Nut, who each evening swallowed the sun so as to give birth to it again in the morning. This last is an image well-known from the New Kingdom: Nut in the form of a woman with an arched body whose hands and feet touch the ground, while her torso, sprinkled with stars, represents the vault of the sky. But what indication authorizes us to read this realistic figure from more than a thousand years later back into the geometric forms of these pillars? Viewing the entire solar cycle as symbolized by the pillars of the temple, these scholars conclude that as early as Dynasty 4, the Sphinx played a solar role in the form of Khepri-Re-Atum, that the temple was dedicated to him, and that he answered to the name Harmakhis, though we have no attestation of this name from before the New Kingdom. This dubious interpretation was pointedly critiqued by Rudolf Anthes, who insisted that this Old Kingdom building cannot be called a temple of Harmakhis; he saw it as a first attempt at a temple dedicated to the solar cult of Re, not Horus-in-the-horizon, while the Sphinx symbolized the sovereign presenting offerings intended for the altar. Though it is much more restrained, Anthes' explanation also goes beyond what can be advanced without falling into unverifiable hypotheses. The same is true of connections with the primordial god Atum, who was linked with Harmakhis only at a much later date.

To end with a still unresolved question, I shall content myself with stating that the Sphinx was modeled as a gigantic image of Chephren, who as pharaoh was endowed with a divine office during life and, of course, after death as well. This statue has no equal, and the temple constructed in front of it, which is also unique, surely had a connection with the colossus: but what? Egyptologist Barry Kemp has submitted the Egyptological style of thinking to an acerbic critique that is not without humor. He justly stresses that although we are sometimes in a position to develop a type of reasoning like that of the ancient Egyptians, if we begin with hypotheses that are not solidly established, they yield solutions that can only be conjectural. Taking up the specific question of the interpretation of the Sphinx temple, he concludes, not without irony, that if we could contact the Egyptians of that period, they could answer "yes" or "no" to a hypothesis that has been proposed. Yet they also might agree that they had not thought of a certain interpretation, but that in fact the suggestion was acceptable to them. Kemp's point underlines the fact that the Egyptian theological system was not closed, but rather open. Still, we cannot be better theologians than the Egyptians themselves. To try to write our own "ancient" theology would be to exceed the limits of interpretation.

5

The Transformations of the New Kingdom

At the beginning of the New Kingdom, during the reign of Amenophis I, a renewal at Giza began that reached its highest points under Amenophis II and Tuthmosis IV, and then again in Dynasty 19 with Ramesses II. The site, which had been rapidly invaded by sand, had been abandoned or nearly abandoned for more than five centuries. Its appearance must have been like that encountered by travelers in the nineteenth century. The cemeteries of royal officials of the Old Kingdom must have seemed like a series of hills and valleys hiding the mastabas. The temples associated with the pyramids had already been plundered and then gradually disappeared under the sand along with the depression of the Sphinx, whose head was one of the only elements still visible, along with the pyramids. One can only wonder about this renaissance of the plateau, which was used for ends that differed entirely from those of the Old Kingdom. The site was no longer a royal and private necropolis attached to the capital city Memphis, but rather a cult place and a place of pilgrimage whose heart was the Great Sphinx, henceforth known by the name Haremakhet. Before investigating the reasons for this transformation, it is indispensable to supply an account of the historical and religious contexts within which these changes took place. Giza was not an isolated site with no relation to the general evolution of the apex of the delta.

MEMPHIS IN THE NEW KINGDOM

As in the past, close bonds linked the Giza plateau to the metropolis of the north, about twenty miles away. From Memphis to Abu Rawash, the edge of the western desert and the alluvial plain constituted a unique entity that belonged administratively to the nome (administrative district) of the "White Wall" (a name of Memphis); the area also had relations with another major city a bit farther north, Heliopolis, which heavily influenced the religious concepts of the Egyptians. Memphis had experienced a marked decline in the Middle Kingdom, and thus later than the decline of Giza as a royal cemetery. The focus of interest had turned to Thebes, a small town that rose to prominence under the sovereigns of Dynasty 11. After the reconquest of Egypt from the Hyksos by Ahmose and the beginning of Dynasty 18, this situation changed. For too long, the attention of historians and archaeologists has been attracted by Thebes, which became the official, political, and administrative capital of the entire land. Though Thebes was not their permanent residence, the New Kingdom pharaohs had themselves buried there in tombs cut into the rock for that purpose. The cult of Amun of Thebes, once local and insignificant, supplanted that of Montu, which had been the more important one in the Middle Kingdom. Amun became a sort of "national" god, associated with the cult of the sun in the form of Amun-Re, and was provided with a clergy whose power and influence extended far beyond his temple, which itself constantly grew at the initiative of the sovereigns. We can understand how New Kingdom Memphis remained long out of favor with scholars. The ruin fields of Memphis, present-day Mit Rahina—a colossus, scattered fragments of dismantled temples, their lower parts often in water because of a rise in the water table, plus shattered remains of constructions of unbaked brick—cannot bear comparison with the prestigious monuments of Luxor, Karnak, and the west bank of Thebes. Notwithstanding the finds made in the nineteenth century on the plateau of Saqqara, fixation on the Old Kingdom led to the neglect, until the 1970s, of the Memphite necropolis' immense store of New Kingdom monuments. This state of affairs can be summarized by the deceptive equation Memphis = Old Kingdom, Luxor = New Kingdom. We now better understand the political and administrative workings of Egypt, which always required a vital center in the north to control the delta, which was too distant from Thebes. Meanwhile, various finds have been gradually fattening our dossier on Memphis in the New Kingdom. The present-day landscape is deceptive, for it in no way corresponds to the historical reality that emerges from Egyptian documents. The city, whose beauty and pleasant lifestyle were praised in literary texts and scribal correspondence, also played an indisputable political, military, administrative, economic, and religious role.

The sovereigns of the New Kingdom conducted many military campaigns into the Near East. Because of its location, Memphis was the favored point of departure for such expeditions. The city was thus provided with a garrison that had an arsenal for the manufacture of weapons. In addition, a civilian and military river port, Peru-nefer (good departure), flourished particularly under Amenophis II and Tuthmosis IV. When Ramesses II reorganized the divisions of his army, one of them bore the name of Ptah, the patron deity of the city. In addition to its military function, Memphis served as the administrative and economic capital of northern Egypt until it found itself in competition with Pi-Riamsese, the royal seat founded by Ramesses II in the northeast delta. Royal domains managed by great stewards were created by various monarchs. Royal decrees issued at Memphis attest that the pharaohs lived in that city far from Thebes, at least on a seasonal basis. Royal jubilees—commemorations of their coronation—also were celebrated there, as under Ramesses II and Ramesses III. The kings often sent their sons, both their eldest sons, designated to succeed them, and any younger sons, to their northern domains to exercise their royal prerogatives and to receive their training as heirs to the throne. Many documents from Giza, including the stela of Tuthmosis IV, attest to this tradition. At this time, Memphis enjoyed an unequaled heyday as a cosmopolitan city where Egyptians mingled with people from the Near East. Both for military reasons, as prisoners were brought back from military campaigns, or as the result of the numerous economic exchanges with western Asia, a foreign population became settled in the various quarters of Memphis, so that the city experienced a certain ethnic mingling. Egyptians with a taste for the exotic flocked there, where they could enjoy imported luxury items, chariot riding, and training in the use of horses, unknown in the Egyptian army prior to the Hyksos conquest.

They also began incorporating Semitic words in their vocabulary. Men of Near Eastern origin, who no doubt had quickly become Egyptianized, occupied important offices, and with the title "butler," they could become devoted servants of the pharaoh, especially under Ramesses III.

This phenomenon of acculturation also occurred in the domain of religion. Beginning with the reign of Amenophis II, side by side with the traditional gods and goddesses, we see the establishment and spread of the worship of the Syro-Palestinian deities Reshep, Astarte, and Baal, to whom sanctuaries were dedicated in various parts of the city. These deities were known to Egyptians as the result of their many contacts with foreign lands at this time. But it is likely that their cults were organized by the initiative of the pharaohs, as indicated by their mention in royal documents, such as the naming of Reshep and Astarte on the stela of Amenophis II at Giza. The case of Haurun is a special one. He, too, was a Canaanite deity, and his earliest attested place of worship is Giza, where he was associated with the figure of Harmakhis and his various epithets. We find him under the newly created composite name of Haurun-Harmakhis, the only case of the combining of a foreign god with an Egyptian deity. This phenomenon began in the reign of Amenophis II, and it continued until the end of the native dynasties.

Nor were the traditional cults neglected, such as that of Ptah, whose temple experienced successive modifications and enlargements. This Memphite god was often associated with Sokar and Osiris, who are found in the neighborhood of Giza. The cults of Hathor, Sakhmet, and the Apis (the sacred bull of Memphis) grew in popularity, especially that of Apis. The first known burials of this sacred animal date to Amenophis III, and the Serapeum, the cemetery of the Apis bulls at Saqqara, was completely reorganized by Khaemwese, son of Ramesses II and high priest of Ptah. Throughout this period, Saqqara witnessed the growth of a remarkable cemetery that sheltered the remains of important persons, including Aperia, a vizier under Amenophis III; Maya, steward of the treasury in the reign of Tutankhamun; the general Haremhab, who rose to the throne; and Tia and Tia, the sister and brother-in-law of Ramesses II.

Despite the dilapidated condition of the ruins of Memphis they contain the remains of a glorious past whose records were stored in the annals preserved by the Egyptians. A veritable reinterpretation of the site now occurred. We need only add, as a counterweight to the role of Memphis, the role played by Heliopolis in the elaboration of the deity Horus-in-the-horizon, whose marked solar coloration becomes clear from an analysis of the stela of Tuthmosis IV. Archaeologically, Heliopolis is even less well-known than Memphis. We nevertheless have a relatively precise idea of the theology that was elaborated around the creator god Atum, who continued to be associated with the sun god Re even after the spread of the cult of Amun. In the middle of Dynasty 18, theologians appealed to these solar concepts as a counterpoint to Amun's power, well before the episode of the heresy of Amarna. These religious ideas were utilized in the development of the figure of Harmakhis as it was forged during Dynasty 18.

THE ROYAL UNDERTAKINGS

It would be unrealistic to think that ordinary private persons, even persons of high rank, would have inaugurated a cult devoted to the Sphinx. The transformations we observe were the fruit of royal initiatives and undertakings, as is amply confirmed by the documents found at the site. This circumstance in no way prevented the parallel multiplication of objects testifying to personal devotion that individuals from various social groups would come to dedicate to the Sphinx.

An early piece, a minuscule base intended for a statue that has disappeared, attests to the association of King Amenophis I, the founder of Dynasty 18, with the name of the Sphinx, Harmakhis. Nevertheless, we are in no position to make suggestions regarding the works that might have been undertaken at the beginning of the dynasty. Amenmes, chief general and eldest son of Tuthmosis I, dedicated a small limestone naos[1] bearing the name of Harmakhis, whose text evokes what would become a *topos* in royal inscriptions: the prince went for a ride, which, according to more explicit documents, meant going from Memphis to Giza and stopping in

---

[1] Egyptologists use this Greek term to indicate two different things. One is the room at the back of a temple, its "holy of holies," which shelters the statue of the god of the temple. The other is a portable object of stone or wood that is also intended to contain a divine effigy. The word is employed here in the latter sense.

the vicinity of the Sphinx. It is likely that even before the reign of Amenophis II, efforts were made to clear the sector from the sands.

Amenophis II initiated major operations to make the area around the Sphinx, the temenos at the foot of the causeway of Chephren, into a veritable sanctuary. In 1936, Selim Hassan uncovered a chapel of unbaked brick northeast of the colossus, aligned precisely with the axis of its head. The doorjambs and lintels were made of fine limestone, which was also used to encase the brick walls of the chapel. This chapel, dedicated to Harmakhis as stated in the inscriptions on its doorways, was intended to shelter a monumental limestone stela—more than 13 feet high by 11½ feet wide—bearing the name of Amenophis II. The stela is preserved *in situ*, accompanied by a second, much smaller one, a partial doublet of the first. Numerous votive objects also were found there, including sphinxes and lions, one of which still lay beside the entrance at the moment of discovery. The building overhangs the depression of the Sphinx, for it was built on a level corresponding to the roof of the Dynasty 4 temple known as the Sphinx temple.

A long text of twenty-seven lines is carved on the stela. It has often been commented on, especially in calculations of the length of the coregency regency between Amenophis II and his father, Tuthmosis III. It also offers valuable information regarding the king's intentions regarding the Sphinx. At the top, in the lunette, the Sphinx is represented twice, to the left and to the right, facing the king, who is making ritual offerings. Below, we read: "the boyhood of the king." The first eleven lines of text are devoted to a traditional eulogy of the new king, for the stela, which bears no date, was probably set up shortly after his coronation. Next, the text enumerates the kinds of physical exercise to which the prince devoted himself at the age of eighteen—footracing, regattas, archery, breaking in horses, chariot racing—in a hyperbolic style conforming to this genre, briefer examples of which can be found in contemporary texts. Some scholars have maintained that these exploits are to be connected with the king's coronation, but this is scarcely compatible with the organization of the text. The prince received his training not to be king, but to be head of the army, much to the satisfaction of his father. The end of the account offers the key to the entire text. Without anyone's knowledge, Amenophis took his horses, which belonged to the stables of Memphis, and went to the plateau of Giza; there he contemplated the Sphinx and the pyramids of Cheops and Chephren and experienced a desire to "make their names live," which was a duty of sons toward their father and toward ancestors more generally. This vow remained secret; he fulfilled it when he ascended the throne:

> Then his majesty remembered the place where he had enjoyed himself near the pyramids of Harmakhis. It was commanded that a way station be constructed there. A stela of white stone was set up there. Carved on it was the great name of Akheprure, beloved of Harmakhis, given life forever.

The erection of the stela and the construction of the chapel, both of them intended to honor the Sphinx, commemorated a prior visit and permitted the name of Harmakhis to be "made to live," and by this means, those of the builders of the pyramids as well. The text of the stela tells a story within a story, a recollection going back to the remote antiquity of the site: proud of his athletic exploits, the king took advantage of this opportunity to boast of them, stressing that they took place in the framework of the Memphis region, although that was not the principal intent of the stela's commemoration.

Some questions arise with regard to this clearing of the area around the Sphinx. Tuthmosis IV boasted of having cleared the Sphinx from the sand, but the operation could have had an earlier start. Amenophis II's activities took place in the framework of a clearing of the sector; furthermore, the Sphinx is represented in its entirety on Amenophis' stela, resting on a base, as on several slightly older stelae. That evidence thus suggests a clearing that began before the reign of Amenophis II and culminated during that of Tuthmosis IV. The other problem is the date of the appearance of the name Haurun at Giza. We find it on the stela of a certain Mes, who might date to the reign of Tuthmosis III, and on foundation plaques from the chapel of Harmakhis. Their texts, rather badly written in black ink, have generated a great deal of discussion. It seems, though, that we can see the double name Haurun-Harmakhis written on them, along with that of Harmakhis alone. Added to this question is the controversy concerning the colossal statue between the forelegs of the Sphinx. In fact, among the six stelae that display this image, at least three date to this period: they belong to three princes, among whom only one, Amenemope, is not anonymous. The princes dedicated these stelae to the Sphinx during the reign of Amenophis II, whose cartouches are carved in front of the statue.

Whether Tuthmosis IV legitimately succeeded his father—a topic of much quibbling among historians—he proved to be a worthy successor at Giza. He rivaled his predecessor with activities that considerably changed the appearance of the Sphinx temenos, known as Setepet, "the chosen place." Among the good thirty documents that are preserved, his Sphinx Stela is indubitably the masterpiece. This monument of pink granite, 12 feet high by more than 6½ feet wide—dimensions worthy of the size of the Sphinx—was recut into an Old Kingdom lintel and was set up between the forelegs of the Sphinx. In the upper register, as on the stela of Amenophis II, we find a representation of two recumbent sphinxes, back to back, on a tall base, to whom Tuthmosis is offering, respectively, incense and libation and a water ewer. The text consists of twenty lines, of which the last are filled with lacunae caused by erosion, a circumstance that has opened the door to hazardous interpretations. Because of spellings of words that are rare and sometimes erroneous, the stela was at one time considered apocryphal, a theory that has been abandoned. Dated to year 1, it is a document from the youth of the king. It employs a literary technique—setting forth an anecdote, real or fictitious—that underlies the genre known as Königsnovelle (royal novel), in which history is mixed with panegyric. The text begins with a traditional encomium, with a Heliopolitan influence shown by the gods who are invoked: Re, Harakhty, Khepri, and Atum. Then, several sentences review the king's physical exercises and hunting activities, which took place around the Setepet of Harmakhis; these lines supply us with a valuable topographical list of cult places in the vicinity. The text then divulges the unique fact, the extraordinary event that both explains and justifies the later deeds of the new king:

> One day, it happened that the royal son Tuthmosis took a walk at the hour of noon and seated himself in the shade of this great god (i.e., Harmakhis). Sleep and dream seized him at the moment when the sun was at its zenith. He saw that the majesty of this august god was speaking

with his own mouth, as a father speaks to his son: "Behold me; cast your gaze on me, o my son Tuthmosis. It is I, your father Harmakhis-Khepri-Re-Atum. I shall give you my kingship on earth at the head of the living. . . . See, my condition is that of a suffering being, as my entire body is in a state of ruin. The sand of the desert on which I stand has encroached upon me. I hasten to entrust to you the realization of what is in my heart, for I know that you are my son, my protector. Approach; see, I am with you, it is I who am your guide.

Despite its lacuna-ridden condition, the end of the text enables us to understand that upon awakening, the prince, astonished by this miracle, kept silent about what he had heard; but we lack what we would expect, confirmation that the project was carried out. This omission is purely a matter of the condition of the text, for the setting up of the stela is direct proof that Tuthmosis undertook work in the sanctuary of Harmakhis. The text, which is far from being without poetry, is not, strictly speaking, a prophetic dream. It envisions the possibility of a face-to-face encounter between the prince and the god himself, something that could not occur in a waking state; Egyptian deities were unapproachable and appeared only under exceptional circumstances. Harmakhis presents himself as the father of the young heir, to whom he promises the royal office, and asks him—not in exchange, but as a filial duty—to save his statue from ruin and from its buried condition. This dream has often been interpreted in too unequivocal a manner, as indicating a necessity for Tuthmosis IV to legitimate his assumption of the throne by means of a divine decree. The insistence on divine filiation is crucial, and the choice of Harmakhis rather than Amun indicates the importance accorded to the former; however, these facts do not authorize a conclusion that we are dealing with a stratagem to dissimulate an illegitimacy. Quite the contrary: Tuthmosis flatters himself that he received, along with the office of kingship, an order issued by the god asking his aid; he would have felt a pressing duty to carry out what had been asked of him, and he kept the matter secret. If we compare the texts of father and son, Amenophis II and Tuthmosis IV, they display striking analogies in their composition. The young prince frequents the Giza plateau during his years of training, when he resides at Memphis. Once he becomes king, he commemorates his visits with construction work or renovations, thus honoring the prestigious deity Harmakhis. Tuthmosis distinguishes himself from his father in that he is invested with a mission entrusted to him by the god himself and does not act merely from a desire to make a pious commemoration.

There is little doubt that he in fact proceeded to make a general clearing of the Sphinx temenos, for sections of walls of unbaked brick dating to his reign still survive. These walls served to protect the Sphinx and, secondarily, could be studded with royal stelae and private ex-voto offerings testifying to the devotion that Harmakhis received. The stelae include a series of seventeen depicting Tuthmosis IV, sometimes accompanied by his wife Nefertari, performing ritual offerings before deities, many of whom presided over local cults cited in the list from the Sphinx Stela. It is as though we see a desire to place the colossal statue at the center of the constellation of locales in the neighborhood.

Another conservation measure was the restoration of the body of the statue itself, as requested by the god in the prince's dream. The Sphinx had already suffered badly from erosion. The first of the three phases of repairs highlighted above is attributable to Tuthmosis IV and was contemporary with the erection of his stela and the protective walls. With the help of large limestone blocks from Tura, which would have covered the entire surface, the eroded body of the animal would have once again assumed the form of a lion, with perhaps even some color and some decorative motifs, such as those in the representations on the stelae. The repair of the uraeus that surmounted the *nemes* supposedly also dates to this period. This dating is plausible, for it corresponds to a time of intense efforts; however, it remains conjectural, and Dynasty 19 cannot be excluded. To complete the reorganization plan, Tuthmosis IV likely ordered the construction of a stairway leading down to the Sphinx, which was covered over at a much later date by the monumental stairs of the Roman Period. At the top of the stairway, a limestone platform faced the Sphinx; the doorjamb and cavetto cornice found nearby could have belonged to this kiosk.

Among the pieces from his reign, two fragments stand out. They belonged to a statue of the king's mother, Tia. In addition to a mention of Harmakhis to invoke his blessing on the queen, the latter's titulary curiously includes the reappearance of titles that had vanished by this period. This phenomenon leads us to think that ancient models were perhaps being investigated at that time, with the intent of bringing the past back to life, and with the taste for archaism that we can follow through the history of Egypt.

We have much less information about the Sphinx from the second part of Dynasty 18. Perhaps the site was somewhat neglected by the sovereigns of the period. Nevertheless, there are traces of a building erected by Tutankhamun southwest of the valley temple of Chephren, on the other side of his causeway. The walls of unbaked bricks stood many feet tall when the edifice was uncovered; now all that remains is a limestone door inscribed with the name of the pharaoh, beloved of Haurun. The building was later usurped by Ramesses II. The rectangular structure was oriented north-south and contained eleven rooms on each side of a central corridor, one of which had a basin for the drainage of water. Just east of the valley temple a construction similar to the "villas" of the Amarna Period was discovered, but it too was later destroyed. It might have been the remnant of a vast residential complex, intended for the pharaohs and their retinues, that was constructed south of the Sphinx; we have examples of these from other sites in Egypt. The building could have remained in use down to the Ramesside Period, for the door was reused by Ramesses II.

Dynasty 19 evinced a renewed interest in the sanctuary and cult of Harmakhis. Sethos I repaired and renovated the chapel of Amenophis II; the principal door leading into the temple bears Sethos' name on the thicknesses of its jambs. Outside, on the doorposts, the cartouches are those of Merneptah, the successor of Ramesses II. Undoubtedly in imitation of the sovereigns of Dynasty 18, a stela was erected in the second principal room of the temple. Though it is badly deteriorated, we can still make out three registers. The first, which is today totally effaced, probably contained a double representation of Harmakhis, in imitation of the other documents of this type. The middle section contains a hunting scene, which is without parallel on similar monuments. On foot, the king shoots a number of animals, as confirmed by the text, which notes the killing of a lion and mentions military exploits. At the same time, it is clearly specified that Sethos dedicated the stela to Haurun-Harmakhis.

After Tuthmosis IV, Ramesses II is the sovereign who left the most evidence of his activity at Giza, a phenomenon that reflects the widespread construction throughout Egypt during his lengthy reign. Certain documents, such as a stela fragment from year 1, date to the beginning of his reign. After all, Ramesses resided at Memphis in these early years, before the foundation of Pi-Riamsese. Tutankhamun's construction remained in use. The most substantial part of Ramesses' activity, such as we know it, was concentrated in the small temple between the forelegs of the Sphinx, where he completed the work of Tuthmosis IV. Perpendicular to the chest of the animal and the stela of Tuthmosis, Ramesses had two bas-reliefs that faced each other on walls parallel to the legs. The bas-reliefs are now in the Louvre (Figures 8 and 9). Their size is not comparable to that of the aforementioned royal stelae, and their texts are reduced to a minimum. A legend identifies Harmakhis, and labels accompany the actions of the king—making offerings, censings, or libations. Finally, some epithets are attributed to the pharaoh. If Ramesses did not deem it appropriate to mention a visit to the plateau of Giza, the collection of stelae is no less skillfully organized. The two sphinxes face east, like the colossus itself, which made it possible to depict the king facing the Sphinx, master of the locale; just as in a temple, the pharaoh proceeds from the exterior toward the holy of holies. If we compare the totality of the iconography of the three monuments, we perceive its remarkable coherence. The Sphinx rests on the same type of tall base with a palace façade decoration related to that of sarcophagi from the Old Kingdom. The Sphinx is represented with a simple *nemes* and a divine beard. The pedestal tables serving as offering stands in front of it are quite similar. Both Tuthmosis IV and Ramesses II wear short kilts with starched triangular frontal pieces and the same headdresses, the blue crown and the *nemes*. Despite stylistic peculiarities due to the different periods, and bas versus raised relief, the small naos was supposed to seem to be a whole chapel, with Ramesses' reliefs resting on their supports at the same height as that of the images of the Sphinx on the stela of Tuthmosis. Further, they were painted red, like a number of votive objects found in the neighborhood; this color was the means of making limestone imitate granite. This balance was not the result of chance; it testifies to an intent to create, between the forelegs of the Sphinx, a sort of open-air naos dedicated to it. As for the beard and the uraeus, the hypothesis that they were restored in Dynasty 19 rather than in Dynasty 18 must be posed, though no clear evidence enables us to choose one over the other.

Figure 8. Stela depicting Ramesses II offering to the Sphinx. Louvre B 18. © Chuzeville.

After Ramesses II, documentation becomes sparse. We know of a door-post bearing the name of Ramesses III, found near the chapel of Amenophis II, and of scattered documents, a situation that conforms to the poverty of other sites from Dynasty 20. The New Kingdom seems to have been a period of intense activity around the Sphinx, which was regularly cleared and then covered again by the sands that would return to attack it. At this time it was entirely restored, with a casing of limestone that hid the damage that erosion had inflicted upon its body and forelegs. The monument was surrounded by a series of chapels between its forelegs and overhanging it, along with stelae bearing the names of pharaohs who promoted its worship. Meanwhile, all of it was protected, like a temple, by a wall of unbaked brick with an access from the northeast that permitted a descent into the depression where the colossus lay. The documents we have reviewed present Harmakhis as protector of royalty and object of a devotion that included reverence toward the site of Giza, whose antiquity was recognized.

Figure 9. Stela depicting Ramesses II offering to the Sphinx. Louvre B 19. ©
Chuzeville.

PERSONAL DEVOTION

The undertakings as vast as those carried out around the Sphinx could
only have been the result of royal initiative, if only because of the material
means they required; even so, this in no way suggests that private individuals were excluded from the cult of Harmakhis. Dozens of texts testify to
the contrary. The *Setepet* of Harmakhis received tokens of piety, of higher
or lower quality according to the social level of the devotee. Cleared and
reorganized, the Sphinx temenos became a place of pilgrimage in the
presence of a god who, unlike most Egyptian deities, was visible to all, for
his statue loomed in the open air and was never hidden. One might conclude that a gap existed between official religion and personal piety such
that individuals were led to address themselves to a single deity of their
choosing within the framework of a polytheistic religion, but this was not
the case. The same deities were worshiped by all. Harmakhis was simply
one of the most accessible deities, for private individuals were kept distant
from the rituals conducted in temples, which were reserved for priests

alone. Thus, as in the case of other sites in Egypt—the Serapeum of Saqqara, the temple of Sakhmet of Sahure at Abusir, south of Giza, and the sanctuaries of Deir el-Medina—we have a coherent assemblage of evidence offering a picture of private religious practices on the plateau of Giza. Study of the documentation facilitates a better understanding of how the god was perceived, while offering other avenues to explore. The names and offices (when indicated) of the persons involved make it possible to determine what kinds of pilgrims visited the Sphinx.

The evidence consists of various artifacts that have generated different degrees of interest on the part of the excavators. There are statuettes of various sizes and different materials, mostly stone or bronze. For the most part, they represent Harmakhis or Haurun-Harmakhis in his traditional sphinx form, but also as a falcon (Figure 10) and thus as a form of Horus, in conformity with the polymorphism of deities. Most often, the statuettes are uninscribed, though sometimes they bear the dedication "made by (so-and-so)." Their stylistic particulars are not explicit enough to date them precisely. They were certainly offered throughout the New Kingdom, and afterward as well. Offering tables, which could have accompanied stelae, have also been found.

It is this last group of about one hundred pieces, some intact and some fragmentary, that supplies the richest information. Unlike with the royal stelae, attributing an exact date to these private stelae is difficult. A small minority of them bear royal cartouches, but most of them do not, and stylistic criteria can be used only with caution in estimating a date, especially in the case of the relatively crude examples. We do not intend to describe these objects individually, but rather to focus on elements that facilitate a general analysis. Through their similarities and their differences, the representations of Harmakhis on these stelae enable us to follow the transformations of the actual statue by means of its various iconographic representations. Moreover, the personages who left these votive objects shed light on the significance of their pilgrimage. The size of the stelae varies from approximately 6 to 28 inches in height, with an average of 12 to 16 inches. They are made from the limestone of uneven quality that is found in abundance in the area; at the moment of discovery, some still bore bright traces of color that subsequently faded with exposure to air. The great majority of them have a rounded top, though a few examples are rectangular.

Figure 10. Haurun-Harmachis (i.e., the Sphinx) represented as a falcon. Cairo Museum, JE 72290. Photo by J.J. Clère.

The god, Harmakhis or Haurun-Harmakhis, is mostly represented as a sphinx—the very image of the colossal statue that the pilgrims encountered on the plateau. In some cases, the sphinx is replaced by a falcon, a form of Horus taken over by Harmakhis, who was himself a local hypostasis of Horus; the falcon was also a representation of the Canaanite Haurun. The god almost always faces right (Figure 11), which is normal for deities on this type of stela and corresponds to the usual direction of writing, which was from right to left. We encounter some exceptions in which the animal faces left, as well as one example with two sphinxes facing each other, and not back to back as on the royal stelae. On many of these monuments, the colossus simply rests on a line that represents the ground, but often he lies recumbent on a base of variable height and which is sometimes adorned with a cavetto cornice. In some cases the middle of the base has what has been described as a door; this is probably a simplified version of the "palace façade" decoration of the royal stelae.

The stela of Benermerut, who lived during the reign of Tuthmosis III, bears a unique image: the Sphinx's base, decorated with a cavetto cornice and a "door," is itself resting on a podium that has a flight of stairs. When compared with reality, this image seems strange, for to approach the Sphinx at that point in time, one had to descend a staircase. We can see from this example that there was no systematic resemblance between the reality of an object and its image. The frequent representation of this base, which scholars already knew from the royal stelae, has raised many questions ever since research began in the temenos of the Sphinx. These representations prompted early excavators, including Maspero, to search for a base that presumably did exist. This exercise was in vain, for the Sphinx and the ground around it form a whole and are part of the rock of the plateau. Selim Hassan suggested that this iconography was a transposition of what was seen by visitors standing in front of the Sphinx, to whom the Dynasty 4 temple seemed to serve as a sort of base. But this explanation loses sight of the fact that at this time, the temple was covered with sand, and that visitors walked across its roof in order to descend toward the statue. We face various questions of interpreting these images: Do the images on the stelae compel us to imagine an ancient reality of which these representations are supposedly a faithful reflection? If so, how are we to explain the diversity of elements that are not mere details? If not, should we take certain iconographic details into account while ignoring others?

Figure 11. Stela of Inhermose depicting the Sphinx. Cairo Museum, JE 72260. Photo by J.J. Clère.

When Egyptian artists made an image in two or three dimensions, whether stelae, bas-reliefs, or statues, their priority was not to observe the principles of realism and correspondence between the image and the entity represented, especially when the work involved a deity characterized by polymorphism. We should be cautious in using such images in arguments intended to re-create an archeological reality that has disappeared. Certain elements in these representations of the Sphinx do indeed correspond to what we find on the statue itself. Hypotheses that are proposed to elucidate the meaning of other elements should take into account the fact that images of a god, whether human, animal, or mixed, were supposed to represent his divine and multifaceted nature, and not his literal appearance.

The Sphinx is most often carved recumbent, his front legs stretched out in front of him, and his tail always visible whether he faces right or left. A few stelae represent him walking—in other words, on all fours and in a striding posture. Occasionally his human head is replaced by that of a falcon, recalling the other form of Harmakhis. Generally, his face is not clean-shaven, but rather is adorned with a beard that is usually plaited and curved at the end. In a dozen cases, we find the beard with a squared end that was worn by kings and royal sphinxes. This variant should not arouse debate, for the preserved remnants of the Sphinx's beard seem to belong to the category of curved beard, and the majority of the representations would thus seem to conform to this reality. The remainder would testify to a liberty taken by the sculptors, who otherwise knew examples of royal sphinxes with squared beards. Moreover, like much of what we have from ancient Egypt, these stelae were rarely the work of experienced artists, and they do not obey immutable figurative rules.

The *nemes*, with its knot visible at the top of the back, is the Sphinx's headdress *par excellence*. Six examples represent it topped by a *pshent*, a combination of the red and white crowns typically worn by kings. In some cases, we find the two-feathered *atef*-crown, which was reserved especially for Osiris, or a composite crown, and in two cases, a sun disk. Some scholars have hypothesized that in the New Kingdom, the Sphinx actually had a crown added to the top of its *nemes*. Archaeologically speaking, that is possible, but it has not been proved. Which of these images are we to trust? The divine epithets corresponding to these representations do not seem to justify these differences. Even if we retain the theoretical possibility of an actual, detachable crown, we must treat these images on their own terms and again suggest that the sculptors found their models in other divine representations.

The body is often covered with a falcon's feathers, an allusion to the other form in which the god could be incarnate. Traces of paint on the casing stones of the animal could attest to the existence of this decoration on the statue itself. The neck is sometimes adorned with the *usekh* collar worn by deities. Finally, on five stelae, the back of the animal is surmounted by a huge flagellum symbolizing an aspect of the divinity of the colossus: it is the shadow of the god that hovers above it. Image and sign were inseparable in Egyptian thought: the flagellum could be a word-sign meaning "shadow," and the shadow was one of the facets making up a personality, whether divine or human.

Among the images of the Sphinx, the thorniest problem is that of the statue represented between the forelegs of the colossus on six of the stelae. It is represented on the three stelae of princes from the reign of Amenophis II, in each case with a base, indicating that it is indeed a question of a statue, and is accompanied in two cases by the cartouches of this king. The three other examples belong to private persons; that of Mes has a cartouche with a dubious reading that could indicate either Tuthmosis III or Tuthmosis IV. The stela of Montuhor, which is rather worn, could belong stylistically to the first half of Dynasty 18, and besides the statue, it bears a unique representation: in the background of the Sphinx, we see the profiles of two pyramids with extremely steep sides, one behind the other as though viewed in perspective, which is rare in Egyptian art (Figure 12). In any case, this image, which highlights the pyramids by associating them with the Sphinx, cannot be viewed as a realistic depiction of the landscape, but rather as a summary of the most prominent features of the site. The final example was dedicated by Tutuia, scribe of the offering table of the Lord of the Two Lands, accompanied by his wife and two brothers. The style suggests the end of Dynasty 18. Two royal figures are depicted, without bases, in front of the legs of the statue (Figure 13). The second figure is indicated by a doubling of the profile by means of a perfectly clean line that cannot be attributed to a change of mind and correction on the part of the sculptor, whose style is far from bad. Perhaps this is a case of the king or his statue along with his *ka*, a life force and

Figure 12. Stela
of the scribe
Montuhor de-
picting pyramids
behind the
Sphinx. Cairo
Museum, JE
72273.Photo by
J.J. Clère.

Figure 13. Stela depicting Tutuia and his family adoring the Sphinx. Between the forelegs is a double representation of a pharaoh. Cairo Museum, JE 72264. Photo by J.J. Clère.

constitutive element of the human personality.[2] We have these images on
the one hand, and on the other, the archaeological object that is the statue
itself. On the chest of the Sphinx, we observe an irregular protuberance.
Many hypotheses have been forged: for example, the remains of a statue
carved in the rock itself and completely eroded, or the back of a naos that
supposedly sheltered a statue. Most recently, Mark Lehner supposedly
found the existence of a colossal statue that would have reached a height
of about 23 feet. Depending largely on the representations just described
to re-create his image of the statue, Lehner proposes to attribute it to
Amenophis II. His reconstruction is plausible, yet it arouses some reserva-
tions. His archaeological arguments might seem irrefutable, but must they
be linked to the images discussed above, utilizing them as evidence of the
reality of that period? If this is the case, it is difficult to understand why
the statue is represented so rarely. Its presence on the stelae is no proof of
its actual existence, for the stela of Tuthmosis IV is never shown, though
doing so would have been possible from an iconographic point of view.[3]
Whether we are being shown a real statue or images of one, the meaning
would be the same: the king is protected by the god, a theme attested
from the same period in sculpture in the round. Do we have a right to use
certain images as proof of what we wish to demonstrate while ignoring
others that do not contribute to the argument? Dynasty 18 might have
witnessed the fabrication of a colossal, independent statue of which not
one trace remains, but the stelae do not necessarily prove its existence.
The protuberance on the chest indicates the existence of a statue that
could have rested against it; any other purpose seems highly unlikely.

In addition to the stelae that depict a falcon, showing that the god
could have multiple images, a series of monuments testifies to personal
piety and the ways in which it could be expressed figuratively. These

[2] This term has sometimes been translated as "double," which does not really correspond
to the rather complex Egyptian concept of a human or divine being, which includes a number of components: *ka*, *ba* (an indestructible life force that permitted mobility in life and in
death), body and corpse, name, shadow.

[3] A painting in an Old Kingdom tomb that was reused in the New Kingdom depicts a
man in adoration before the Sphinx. Represented between its front legs is an object that has
been identified as a stela; this would be unparalleled, however, and it cannot be verified in
the poor reproduction we have at our disposal.

monuments are known as "ear stelae" (Figure 14). These images of human ears accompany the Sphinx, or they are the only thing depicted on the stelae, whether a single ear, a pair of them, or a multiplicity amounting to thirty or more. This type is not specific to Giza. We find ears embellishing stelae dedicated to other deities, such as Ptah at Memphis or Amun at Deir el-Medina. For a long time, these images were mistakenly interpreted. They were viewed as votive objects similar to those once hung in churches to thank God or the saints for a cure, choosing the part of the body that was healed: arm, leg, ear, or other organ. But texts accompanying the Egyptian ears refer to the god "who hears prayers"; the ears thus symbolize both a prayer and an assurance that the god will hear it and show his compassion.

On the more elaborate stelae, the devotee had himself portrayed, alone or with members of his family or a companion whose relationship to him is unknown. Clothing varies according to period and occupation,[4] from a simple kilt to the ample pleated robes of the Ramesside Period. The stelae are organized in two ways. One is a single register that occupies the entire surface, with the dedicator represented facing the Sphinx. The other consists of two registers. The Sphinx is above, while below, we see the dedicator and his relatives, except where they are distributed between the two registers. The gestures of the persons depicted are stereotyped. In most examples, whether they are standing or kneeling, they raise their hands as a sign of adoration, carry large bouquets, and more often still, hold a censer for burning incense. Aside from flowers in abundance, the offering tables are heaped with meat and vegetables offered to the Sphinx. After an adoration of the god, who is endowed with various epithets, the faithful formulate their inscribed wishes with traditional phrases, requesting life, health, strength, love, intelligence, long life, a goodly burial after a lengthy old age, the praise and favor of the god—these are the very words employed in the inscriptions—as well as a share of the offerings presented to the Sphinx. Whatever deity the Egyptians invoked, we find the same wishes for well-being, such as the Egyptians conceived of it on earth and in the afterlife. Only the stelae of the wealthy display these texts. Less for-

---

[4] Thus, a soldier can be recognized by his distinctive loincloth and standard, while a scribe carries his equipment slung over his shoulder.

Figure 14. Stela depicting a devotee kneeling before the Sphinx. The thirty-two ears in the lunette of the stela are intended to encourage the god to listen attentively to prayers. Cairo Museum, JE 72281. Photo by J.J. Clère.

tunate persons had to make do with a "made by so-and-so," while the poorest left an uninscribed stela or a small object in the form of a sphinx or a lion.[5]

A large range of people demonstrated their piety before the *Setepet* of the Sphinx by having stelae set into the unbaked brick walls that protected it. Certain otherwise known high officials signaled their visits: Benermerut, who was chancellor, overseer of the treasury, and overseer of all the works of the king under Tuthmosis III; and from the same reign, Minnakht, noble and count, confidant of the king in the entire land, royal scribe, and overseer of the granaries. These men, who were attached to the court at Thebes, must have traveled regularly to Memphis for official reasons and even made stays there. In the reign of Tuthmosis IV, Iuity was royal butler and child of the *kap*, a military institution. May, overseer of all the works of his majesty Ramesses II, left graffiti near the pyramid of Chephren and also paid his respects to the Sphinx. In the same period, Amenwahsu, scribe of the offering table, made a visit and paid homage to both Haurun-Harmakhis and Ptah-Sokar-Osiris, resident in Rasetau. Various kinds of craftsmen are represented by several members of their group: Hatiay, chief sculptor under Sethos I; Djehutinakht, chief sculptor; Hernefer, chief mason; Amenneb, goldsmith and sculptor. We can imagine that these individuals put their talents to practice at Giza, where workshops were organized to meet the demand for votive objects, but they might have lived at Memphis. We also find evidence of soldiers, some of whom were stationed in the same city: Mes, standard-bearer of the great company; Amenneb, overseer of Nubian troops; Kheruef, standard-bearer of the company "Amun Is the Strength of the Army." The presence of relatively low-ranking military men on this type of document is not the result of chance. In the population at large, they were among those who had the most opportunity to travel. Scribes, the very symbol of the Egyptian administration, also are present: Tutuia, who has already been mentioned;

---

[5] One category of objects we might have expected to find is absent: statues. We find them in temples, where the faithful had the privilege of setting up an effigy of themselves. Perhaps stelae were preferred to statues because this was not a temple in the classical sense. Still, the phenomenon should be noted, especially because in the Late Period, private people left statues at Giza though they are not numerous.

Yuyu, scribe of the double granary of the palace; an anonymous scribe of works in the temple of Ptah; Iahmes, a *wab* (pure) priest and scribe of Hathor, Mistress of the Sycamore; and the scribes Tjur, Montuher, and Kanakht.

Other persons held minor offices in the administration of Memphis. Officials of small neighboring locales also paid a visit: Amenemheb, mayor of Pi-Hapy on the opposite bank of the Nile; Teku, mayor of Maaty in the plain of Giza; a servant who was a native of Kher-Aha (Babylon), where present-day Old Cairo is located; and another servant, Sapair, attached to the temple of Sopdu in the two mounds just north of Giza. Among the rather humble people who left a monument, we note a goatherd named Maa, who had himself represented with a kid in his arms.

This picture is quite revealing. While kings and their sons were attached to the site of Giza, high officials of the realm were few in number—unless, of course, all their monuments have perished. For the most part, it was people in the vicinity, from Memphis in the south to Letopolis and Kher-Aha in the north, who came to visit the Sphinx. This was not a case of "national" pilgrimage, in imitation of Abydos, the holy city of Osiris. The people we encounter are soldiers, scribes, minor officials, employees, artisans, and foremen. As always in Egypt, it was necessary to have a position, even at the bottom of the social ladder, in order to leave a commemorative monument. Peasants, weavers, potters, bakers, and butchers are absent. This does not imply that they felt no devotion to their local god; they were simply among the millions of anonymous individuals who peopled Egypt throughout its history.

Let us try to imagine ourselves on the plateau of Giza during the New Kingdom. The village of Rasetau, which is mentioned on a stela of Ramesses III, lay in the plain beneath the plateau, where present-day Nazlet el-Simman is located. Along with the traditional life of an Egyptian town, which was primarily agricultural, the village had all sorts of activities associated with the cult of the Sphinx: stonemasons and sculptors creating stelae and statues, metalworkers casting objects of bronze, mass producing votive objects or manufacturing them to order, and merchants selling food and incense to be offered to the colossus. The relatively strict organization of the cult was surely balanced by the joyous disorder that must have reigned in this village to which the pilgrims flocked, rather like that in the common quarters of contemporary Egypt during the days of feasting after Ramadan.

THE INVENTION OF A GOD:
THE ROLE AND CULT OF HARMAKHIS

Our historical and sociological approach enables us to marshal the information at our disposal and to reflect on the nature of the god that the Sphinx became at the beginning of the New Kingdom. The evidence indeed presents him as a god, both in his iconography and in the name and epithets that accompany his representations. Beginning with Dynasty 18, the Egyptian name Haremakhet (Greek Harmakhis), "Horus-in-the-horizon," designated the Great Sphinx of Giza, and only the Sphinx. In a number of scholarly works, this name has been incorrectly used in place of that of Harakhty, "Horus-of-the-double-horizon," in contexts that have nothing to do with the Sphinx. The name Harmakhis does not appear until the reign of Amenophis I, and it is entirely unjustified to speak of this god or his name in the Old Kingdom. We have no reason to attribute the god's sudden appearance to the loss of earlier documents that might once have existed. We have no reference to the Sphinx in documents from the Old Kingdom, and during the Middle Kingdom the site of Giza was almost entirely abandoned.

We are thus faced with a religious phenomenon that is entirely original, though not unique: a theological reinterpretation turned an existing statue into the image of the god who had been invented on its basis; the result is that the images of the Sphinx on the stelae are images of an image. This is the opposite of the usual situation. We cannot know the origin of some deities that Egyptians endowed with many iconographic forms. In this reversed circumstance, one fact has persisted: Harmakhis was the Sphinx, and only the Sphinx, and we do not encounter this god in any other form. This fact, however, did not prevent theologians from associating the names of other solar deities with the Sphinx, playing on the name of Horus, which was a part of the Sphinx's name. Another fact distinguishes the Sphinx: Harmakhis, the Sphinx of Giza and the prototype of every other kind of sphinx in Egypt, always retained his specific identity, thus distinguishing this colossus from all other sphinx statues.

It is difficult to explain the birth of this god and the invention of his name, both of which occurred during the resurgence of Memphis. This colossal head rising from the sand between the pyramids of Cheops and Chephren must have impressed those first visitors who proceeded to uncover its body. Perhaps they immediately regarded it as a divine image, one linked to a past that was already ancient, though not entirely buried and forgotten. The name of Cheops, which is not often encountered in texts later than the Old Kingdom, appears on the stela of Amenophis II, along with the name of Chephren. The latter name is also present on Tuthmosis IV's stela, though unfortunately in a context that is badly marred by lacunae. Why was the Sphinx named Horus-in-the-horizon? Did the name Horus originally refer to the god, who is not normally represented as a lion or a sphinx, or did the name originally recall the king, who was also designated Horus? Whichever the case, the combining of deities, which was an Egyptian specialty, showed that Harmakhis was felt to be a form of the god Horus; for this reason the image of the Sphinx was sometimes replaced by that of a falcon. There are various plausible explanations for the term *akhet* ("horizon"); they do not contradict one another, but rather can be juxtaposed according to Henri Frankfort's principle of "multiplicity of approaches." The funerary complex of Cheops was called *Akhet Khufu*, "Horizon of Cheops"; we know at least one mention of it from the Middle Kingdom, showing that it did not fall entirely into oblivion. It is possible that the name was abbreviated as *akhet*, and that this became the general designation of the entire site. Then, the Sphinx could have been called "Horus-in-the-horizon" to give it an explicit designation. As in the case of the god Horus, the word *akhet*, denoting the place where the sun rises and shines, could have led to theological speculation and connections with other solar deities. The position of the Sphinx, facing east and flanked by the two pyramids in the background, would fit this definition wonderfully. The Egyptians did not leave us any explanation of the origin of the name, but these hypotheses seem reasonable, given that they take into account the historical and religious aspects of the context of the birth of Haremakhet.

There was theological play based on the god's name. The Sphinx was also called Harakhty and Re-Harakhty. This assimilation is carried to an extreme in the text on the stela of Tuthmosis IV, at a time when, even before the reign of Amenophis III, growing importance was accorded to the cult of Re, the sun god of Heliopolis. In this text, the Sphinx is presented as the image of Khepri, and then he receives the complex designation Harmakhis-Khepri-Re-Atum, incorporating the triple designation of the sun god as Khepri in the morning, Re at noon, and Atum in the evening. Though their texts are less elaborate, private stelae make this connection between Harmakhis and Atum, which was an essential component of the theological tenets regarding the identity of Harmakhis.

The association of Harmakhis and Haurun, a god of Canaanite origin, is a remarkable and unique religious phenomenon. The name Haurun was long ago noted by Egyptologists, at a time when its attestations were still quite rare; there was an important occurrence on the Stela of the Daughter of Cheops. The name, however, was both misread and misunderstood, and it was taken to be a general term designating the Sphinx, a theory that had to be abandoned. Later, at Tanis, Pierre Montet unearthed an admirable colossal statue of the god in the form of a falcon protecting Ramesses II, who is depicted as a child. The name of the god was clearly legible on the statue, and the connection with the Asiatic deity was made. That was followed by the discovery of stelae in the Sphinx temenos with representations of the colossus bearing the names Harmakhis, Haurun, or Haurun-Harmakhis. The phenomenon assumed some importance: this was not a question of a sporadic and scarcely comprehensible presence, but rather of the establishment of the cult of a foreign god.

At Giza, the earliest attestations of Haurun probably go back to Tuthmosis III and Amenophis II. This was the time when other foreign deities appeared in the region of Memphis; those deities included Reshep and Astarte, whom we find on the stela of Amenophis II. Haurun was thus not an isolated case, but with his installation at Giza, he developed in a direction different from the destiny of other foreign deities who made themselves at home in Egypt. They all became strongly Egyptianized, but they kept their original names. Haurun was the only such deity to see his name either associated with that of the Egyptian god Harmakhis or even replace it as the same of the same image, that of the Sphinx, with no iconographic distinction. Egyptian pharaohs mentioned him: Amenophis II on the foundation plaques of the chapel of Harmakhis; Sethos I in the same chapel; and Tutankhamun, later usurped by Ramesses II in the building south of the Chephren causeway. But although he was introduced at royal initiative, he is found primarily on private stelae, represented as a sphinx and more rarely as a falcon. Down to the Ramesside Period, he remained attached to the site of Giza, and it is only with the reign of Ramesses II that we find him mentioned elsewhere in Egypt, especially at Deir el-Medina, and probably at Pi-Riamsese, with the statue from Tanis cited above. On this statue, the god bears the designation "Ramesses is beloved of Haurun." The royal residence in the delta, which later served as a quarry for the construction of Tanis, is the provenance normally attributed to the statue. There has also been a suggestion that it stems from Giza, where the cult of the god was well established, while he is otherwise unknown from Pi-Riamsese, and there has been a purely theoretical reconstruction of the Sphinx temenos with this statue between the forelegs of the animal. For lack of proof, this possibility can be neither confirmed nor denied.

How are we to explain this phenomenon of extreme acculturation? It is easy to understand that close contacts between Egypt and the Near East facilitated the entry of foreign deities into a constellation of gods and goddesses, for the polytheistic system was open and accommodating. But must we conclude that Syro-Canaanites who had arrived in Egypt, many of them as prisoners of war, were responsible for founding the cults of deities they had brought with them? Such a conclusion seems improbable, even if the Syro-Canaanites were assimilated into the local population. The earliest attestations of Reshep and Astarte are incontestably linked to royal documents, and their chapels in the city of Memphis were built in the temenos of the temple of Ptah or in the quarter of Peru-nefer. Though these deities came from foreign lands, they were immediately adopted by the state, even if they saw their popularity take root in individual devotion. This also seems to have been the fate of Haurun, who would be exclusively linked to the Sphinx of Giza for more than a century. There is also the question of the reason for this quasi-assimilation. The answers, however, are incomplete and insufficient. We have only a vague knowledge of the original nature of this Canaanite god whose attestations in Syria and Palestine and at the site of Ras Shamra antedate those in Egypt by about four centuries. He seems to have been a chthonic god who was also linked to storms and could be invoked in curse formulas. None of these characteristics made him an ideal associate for Harmakhis. A phonetic connection between Hor(us) and Haur(un) has been suggested. This would be an additional reason for the representation of Haurun as a falcon, a form borrowed from Harmakhis. One fact is clear: from Dynasty 18 on, the Sphinx, an entirely Egyptian image, could be invoked by the name of Haurun. And the faithful who called him by that name were not, as has sometimes been unjustifiably claimed, foreigners who were worshiping their god under an Egyptian guise. As shown by their names and their titles, they were Egyptians, or at least completely Egyptianized foreigners.

Under both his names, the god's divinity is proved by the epithets conferred on him, though these are often too common to shed light on his specific aspects. We have no hymn to give us more detailed information about his nature. He is often called "great god," and sporadically we encounter the additional epithet "lord of the sky," which is undoubtedly borrowed from Horus. He is also the "perfect god," the "living god," "ruler of eternity," and sometimes "lord of the desert," which suits his geographical location. In one case, Haurun is called "lord of clouds," which might recall his original role. Kheruef addresses a brief prayer to the god in these terms: "Adoring Harmakhis in his name of Haurun; adoring your beautiful visage. I satisfy your perfection, for you are the unique one who will endure forever, while all men come to their landing (i.e., die). May you grant me a long lifetime, in which I follow your *ka* (i.e., I am faithful to you)." This hymn, on a private stela, is not exceptional as a hymn per se but it is nonetheless touching. In the face of the unchanging divine perfection that the colossal size of the statue undoubtedly conveyed to those who visited the site, this man clearly recognized the transitory nature of the human condition and requested only what he could reasonably hope for and imagine, "a long lifetime."

The Sphinx's attributes include this toponymic epithet: "he who presides over *Setepet*." This word is derived from the root *setep* ("to choose, elect"), and it thus designates his sanctuary as the "chosen place." Because of the special nature of the colossus, an open-air statue visible from all directions, we rarely encounter the classic word for an Egyptian temple, the term *per*, which designates the "house" or "domain" of a deity. In the text on his stela, Amenophis II speaks of a "chapel" of Harmakhis, but the term used in this unique instance is too vague for us to connect it with a specific location at Giza.

Something else that is absent is even more surprising. Chapels were erected in honor of the Sphinx, some of which undoubtedly had storerooms for the items that belonged to every religious foundation, such as jugs of wine; stoppers bearing the name of Amenophis III have been found. Stelae depict the faithful bearing offerings. Even if it were only a matter of demonstrations of personal piety—which is not the case, for kings played an important role at Giza—there had to be specialized personnel attached to the cult places to administer their operations. Yet except for a grain measurer of Haurun named Pay, we have no indication of priests or servants of Haurun-Harmakhis. We can scarcely argue for lost documentation, though that is always possible. Giza has provided so much evidence for the life of the site in the New Kingdom that this lack cannot be merely the result of chance. This circumstance represents a major unknown. The icnography suggests a traditional cult in which offerings, libations, and censings accompanied the prayers, but we do not know whether this worship was carried out daily, like that of the classical temples, or whether special festivals, of which we have no evidence, were celebrated on specific dates. It is in any case unlikely that the Sphinx, which was surrounded by a brick wall, was freely accessible to every individual who came bearing an offering and a votive object. The wall was intended to protect the statue, but it also delimited a sacred space to which access must have been controlled.

Despite the questions that remain, the evidence reveals two roles played by the Sphinx in the form of the god Harmakhis, who was a theological reinterpretation of the New Kingdom. It was peculiar to him that he was in the open air, visible to all, and not hidden in a naos that only priests could approach. In this respect, he resembles the colossal statues at the gates of temples, or those that a sovereign such as Ramesses II commissioned of himself in deified form. The Sphinx would always remain the largest colossus, and it must have aroused admiration, respect, and fear, along with hope of protection. The kings were the first to show interest in the Sphinx, and for them, it would remain a witness to a prestigious and venerable past that they desired to preserve, though the pyramids were left as they were. The Sphinx could have been a guarantor of royal power on a par with Amun, even if his fame scarcely reached beyond Memphis. In a parallel development, at a time when manifestations of personal piety had increased, those excluded from the official cults had, in the case of the Sphinx, the incomparable privilege of "seeing the god," to cite a phrase used by the Egyptians themselves. We thus see the development of a cult of private persons who came to pay homage to the sacred image and to address their requests to it in "the places of prayer of the people," as stated on the stela of Sethos I.

HARMAKHIS AND THE OTHER GODS OF GIZA

We cannot isolate the Sphinx from its context, the plateau of the Great Pyramids, where other cults were founded in the New Kingdom, along with that of Harmakhis. The information at our disposal is fragmentary, in large part because of destruction carried out in antiquity for the purpose of making repairs, and in part because of illicit digging and pillaging in modern times; still, we must try to trace the relationships that might have existed among the deities.

Our first attestation of a cult of the goddess Isis at Giza is from the reign of Amenophis II; on a stela of Prince Amenemope, she is depicted just beneath the image of Harmachis, seated in a naos and receiving her share of the offerings. The votive monuments that Tuthmosis IV undoubtedly had set into the brick wall with which he surrounded the Sphinx included a stela dedicated to her. When Sethos I replaced the doorway of the chapel of Harmakhis, he had a goddess represented facing Re-Harakhty/Harmakhis. Though she is not named, her headdress allows us to presume that she is Isis, who is also present on some of the private stelae. Additionally, faience rings and scarabs inscribed with cartouches of Tuthmosis III, Amenophis III, Tutankhamun, Ay, and Haremhab have been found near the funerary chapel of the pyramid of Henutsen, which was transformed into a temple of Isis in the Third Intermediate Period, or perhaps even earlier. Such small, mass-produced pieces were generally left as votive objects in places of devotion of the sort we call "popular." The cult of Isis, Mistress of the Pyramids, which enjoyed a growing popularity from at least the beginning of Dynasty 21, began in these early manifestations, some of which were instigated by royal initiative. Isis did not at first bear the distinctive epithet that would make her the mistress of the Giza plateau, somewhat displacing Harmakhis in the first millennium. Nevertheless, the two deities were occasionally associated, perhaps because of the relationship between Horus, of whom Harmakhis was a form, and his mother, Isis. Did the faithful who visited the Sphinx temenos also make their way up to the funerary complex of Cheops, where the abandoned chapel of Henutsen's small pyramid had been put back into use? There is too little evidence for us to say more. What is remarkable is the rise of an Isis specific to Giza beginning in Dynasty 18, even if her origin remains unknown. The spread of the cult of Isis was in fact quite limited in this period, though her existence is already attested in the earliest religious texts, where she is connected with the myth of Osiris.

Isis is not mentioned in the long list of deities and cult places on the stela of Tuthmosis IV, which serves as a sort of description of the topography around the Sphinx. We do, however, find Sokar of Rasetau, who enjoys a privileged position, because the *Setepet* of Harmakhis is geographically defined as being "beside Sokar." The same god also receives the epithet "lord of Shetyt" on one of the votive stelae of this pharaoh. The association is again clear on a stela belonging to Amenwahsu from the reign of Ramesses II. Its upper register bears an unusual representation: standing behind Haurun-Harmakhis, "foremost of the *Setepet*," who is represented as a sphinx on a base, we see a falcon-headed god labeled "Ptah-Sokar-Osiris, foremost of the West, the great god who resides in Rasetau." Again under Ramesses, a relief whose likely provenance is Giza depicts a falcon-headed sphinx with the legend "Horus, son of Isis, lord of Rasetau." Several texts bearing the name of Khaemwese, high priest of Ptah in Memphis, mention Osiris of Rasetau. Sokar was an ancient funerary god of the Memphite region who was associated with Rasetau, which is already mentioned in the Pyramid Texts. Rasetau, which means "entrance to the subterranean regions," was not just a part of the mythic geography of the funerary literature: it indicated an actual place in the Memphite cemetery area, undoubtedly south of the Sphinx. Its topography is described rather precisely on the monuments of Khaemwese: Rasetau was composed of two parts, an upper one with its "mountain of upper Rasetau," and a lower one, "the sands," separated by a wadi called "the valley of Rasetau." The village in the plain at the foot of the Sphinx was simply called "the village of Rasetau." Associating deities with one another was a common practice, and Sokar often appears in the composite form of Ptah-Sokar-Osiris, thus connecting him as much with the patron god of Memphis as with Osiris, god of the dead, who eventually supplanted him. In Giza of the Late Period, there are many mentions of Osiris, Lord of Rasetau, and of his temple, though this monument has yet to be found;[6] it is almost certain that it had its beginnings in the New Kingdom.

Was it mere geographical proximity that initially led to the connection between Sokar and Harmakhis? Tuthmosis IV's text gives this impression. Nevertheless, given that the cult of Osiris took root in the locale of Rasetau, it is possible that a bond was formed between Osiris and Horus/Harmakhis, as the legend on the relief of Ramesses II leads us to suppose. Rasetau was an extremely ancient site. From the New Kingdom on, theologians apparently wished to establish connections between the cults at Giza, which were originally separate and originated in very different periods. Since it went back to the Old Kingdom, the cult of Sokar of Rasetau—later replaced by Osiris—was far older than the consecration of the Sphinx as a deity. These relations between Haurun-Harmakhis, Isis, and Osiris were solidly established in the Late Period, as attested by the texts on the Stela of the Daughter of Cheops, but can we simply read this situation back into the New Kingdom? Mariette claimed to have found fragments of a colossal Osirid statue in the area of the masonry heaped up next to the southern flank of the colossus, which could have served as its pedestal. A reconstruction of a naos sheltering this statue has been proposed by Lehner,[7] this naos being the temple of Osiris himself. We must analyze this matter with circumspection. It is possible that an Osirid statue existed in this spot, but the existence of a naos is purely conjectural, and its interpretation as a temple of Osiris is more hazardous still. Archaeolog-

---

[6] Selim Hassan noted that he had found remains of a building southwest of the Sphinx (*The Great Sphinx*, p. 113, n. 1); according to him, this was the temple of Osiris. In reality, the temple has never been found; recently, however, small vases dedicated to Osiris of Rasetau by pharaohs of the New Kingdom have been seen on the antiquities market.

[7] Mark Lehner, *The Great Sphinx*, 368–79 and Figures 9–16, with his alleged reconstruction of the naos, are inspired by the naos still to be seen at the site of Mendes in the delta, but which dates to Dynasty 26.

ical study of the Sphinx has eliminated many unknowns, but it has not enabled us to reconstruct the entire site as it existed in the various phases of its history. Until the end of the New Kingdom, Harmakhis was the uncontested master of the site, with Isis and Osiris still playing only a secondary role.

6

The New Focus of the First Millennium

Though the stela of Tuthmosis IV is famous and often cited, the history of Giza in the New Kingdom is not widely known. The first millennium is even more obscure. The period after the end of the New Kingdom, long regarded as consisting of obscure centuries of decadence, once aroused little interest; even the Saite "renaissance" was considered as a sorry imitation of the glorious days of the Old Kingdom. While it still has its defenders, this unfortunately erroneous view has been gradually corrected. The political reverses of the pharaonic state, which was often broken up into two or more kingdoms, can now be dissociated from the remarkable vitality that manifested itself in the areas of religion and art during the first millennium. Although some zealous partisans of classical Egypt prefer the works of the Old or New Kingdom and treat the admirable statuary of the Late Period with disdain, many scholars today recognize the interest of this period and devote their efforts to publishing the rich documentation it has left us.

Given the older attitude on the part of scholars toward all Egypt in the first millennium, we can easily understand why the evolution of first millennium Giza has remained obscure. The evidence that has come down to us is somewhat unattractive, and pieces were dispersed in museums during the nineteenth century with little attention to their provenance. The objects found by the excavations of the twentieth century have often fallen

into oblivion, relegated to the storerooms of the museums that received a
share of the finds and eclipsed by more spectacular pieces, such as the su-
perb furniture from the tomb of Hetepheres in the cemetery east of the
pyramid of Cheops. This situation corresponds to the concerns underly-
ing early excavations, which centered on uncovering and publishing the
great Old Kingdom cemeteries that constitute the glory of Giza. Further,
the monuments *in situ* present a sorry appearance. Who would visit the
pitiful remains of the temple of Isis, Mistress of the Pyramids, and the constructions associated with it at the foot of the pyramid of Henutsen?

But the situation is less hopeless than it seems at first glance. By taking
into account the elements still in place at Giza, by systematically collecting
the objects found during the nineteenth and twentieth centuries (principally in the Cairo Museum, and in the Museum of Fine Arts in Boston,
which received some of the objects excavated by George Reisner), and by
analyzing unpublished archives (in large part those of the American excavator),[1] it has proved possible to resurrect a whole new segment of the
area's history. That history stretches practically without interruption from
the Old Kingdom on and culminates in the veneration displayed by the
Greeks and then the Romans for the site, especially the Sphinx.

Even in Egypt, history was not static. The first millennium experienced
many reversals, especially on the political level, but also in the domain of
religion. One of the best-known changes was the increasing importance of
the cults of Isis and Osiris, whose clear manifestations at Giza built on
what had begun in the New Kingdom and modified the function of Harmakhis. Though the latter continued to inspire devotion, he was no longer
the dominant figure at the site. Instead, he was part of a complex system of
cults that the priests attempted to organize with a certain coherence.

THE MEMPHITE CONTEXT

To understand the developments at Giza in this period, it is useful to
begin with a brief sketch of the situation in the region. What was the

---

[1] Together with more recent excavations, this patient research in the storerooms at Giza,
in the museums in Cairo and Boston, and in the archives in the latter museum has enabled
me to draw together heretofore unpublished documentation.

function of Memphis during these centuries? What political changes and military defeats did the old capital experience, and what was their impact on the city's religious function? Ramesses II had already shown his preference for the north by creating the new capital of Pi-Riamsese, which survived him, though this development posed no real threat to Memphis. With the end of Dynasty 20, which marked the close of the New Kingdom, substantial changes affected the entire structure of the land. First, Egypt was split in two. While priest-kings descended from the sacerdotal class of the high priests of Amun seized power at Thebes, Smendes, who was succeeded by Psusennes, founded a new capital in the north; this city, Tanis, grew in size and played an important role until the Greek conquest. Since Memphis occupied a crucial place at the apex of the delta, it was not neglected by the sovereigns of the north, whose authority extended that far and even farther south. The temple of Ptah was headed by various members of a local family, though eventually it was entrusted to one of the sons of Osorkon II, a king of Dynasty 22 who reigned at Tanis. His family remained in charge of the temple until the reign of Shoshenq V. Later, power crumbled in the delta during the period of the "Libyan anarchy," which witnessed the creation of autonomous petty kingdoms of various sizes under the rule of Libyan dynasts. At the time of the Kushite invasion from the south, Memphis was conquered by Piye. During the ensuing Dynasty 25, Memphis received attention from the Kushite sovereigns, who gave solicitous support to the cults of both Thebes and Memphis.

With the Saite reconquest, Psammetichus gained control of Memphis. He enlarged the temple of Ptah and inaugurated the subterranean vaults of the Serapeum, where the Apis bulls were regularly buried. When Egypt fell under Persian domination, the city was taken by Cambyses. Archaeological remains contradict the Greek historical tradition that the Persian invaders were irreverent raiders who allegedly killed an Apis: stelae attest that the bull who died in year 6 of Cambyses was buried with the proper rites, and that the tradition continued under Darius. During Dynasty 30, Nectanebo I and II, who commissioned major restorations in many cities, were also active in the ancient capital. After the troubled period of the second Persian domination, the arrival of Alexander the Great was welcomed as a liberation. The three centuries of Greek domination witnessed a great deal of internal difficulty; but the temples and their cults appear to have been maintained and in some cases reorganized, and religious practice remained relatively free of the woes that affected daily life. Though periods of rather intense construction or renovation occurred, the Greek sovereigns in the north seem scarcely to have had the leisure to concern themselves with restoring the temples of the Memphite region. When we encounter names, they usually belong to local dignitaries, especially priests, who worked with their consent and in their stead. We see this phenomenon at Giza as well. The site, which was affiliated with Memphis, had a relatively autonomous life that was organized around the temples of Isis, Mistress of the Pyramids; of Osiris, Lord of Rasetau; and of Harmakhis.

THE TRACE OF SOVEREIGNS

The condition of the pharaonic regime, which became more precarious, affected the pursuit of construction work at Giza. Comparing this era with the New Kingdom, we find far less building activity in the name of the kings who reigned from Dynasty 21 to Dynasty 30. At the site, the center of interest shifted to the pyramid of Henutsen, the southernmost of the three small pyramids, probably those of queens, to the east of that of Cheops. Her funerary chapel, which was undoubtedly already in use in the New Kingdom, was modified and enlarged on a number of occasions—in the reigns of Psusennes and Amenemope in Dynasty 21, and then in Dynasty 26, and perhaps also in the Ptolemaic Period—so as to serve as a temple of Isis. From then on, the goddess bore the epithet Mistress of the Pyramids, which made her the tutelary patron of the Giza plateau. Outside of Tanis, it is at Giza that we encounter the most frequent mention of the first kings of Dynasty 21, though it is uncertain that the transformations of the temple of Isis sprang from a clearly expressed royal desire. They could have been the work of a priest with sufficient influence to act in the name of these kings, a phenomenon that occurred at Memphis with a chapel in the name of Siamun; that chapel was built by Ankhefenmut, a member of the personnel of Ptah.

To judge from the finds, royal works in the area of the Sphinx seem to have been few in number. A fragmentary block of limestone, now in the

Royal Scottish Museum in Edinburgh, bears the two cartouches of Amenemope, who is frequently mentioned in the temple of Isis, as well as a representation of a sphinx wearing a *nemes;* the chin of the sphinx is adorned with a curved beard, and a short cape is draped over its shoulder. Above the animal, a winged *udjat* eye holds an *ankh* sign at the end of an arm. Unfortunately, there is no legend to identify the sphinx with assurance, though many arguments favor a representation of Harmakhis. The image conforms entirely with the many examples we have from the New Kingdom. Further, since the name of Amenemope appears almost nowhere except in Tanis and Giza, this relief likely comes from the latter site. It is perhaps a fragment of a lintel decorated with royal cartouches between a double scene, the rest of which has disappeared. Could it have been part of a building dedicated to Harmakhis under Dynasty 21?

A well-crafted headless statuette of pale green opaque glass represents a kneeling man offering two jars of wine. Part of the collection of the Brooklyn Museum, it reputedly stems from Giza. Carved on the dorsal pillar and the base is a text of the genre known as "appeal to the living": "O all pure priests and all scribes who come to enter the temple, the great god will praise you. . . ." This invocation is made in favor of a certain Smendes, Great Chief of the Ma (a Libyan tribe) and prophet of Amun-Re, Lord of the Horizon. This person seems to have been a local dynast who held office under Dynasty 22 or 23. We should be cautious in interpreting this document. Is the "great god" of the inscription Amun-Re, whose prophet Smendes states that he was? Or is "great god" a particular designation of Harmakhis? Nothing permits us to affirm it, for the text is not sufficiently explicit, and its provenance is questionable. Nevertheless, a point of comparison can be utilized in favor of attributing the statue to Giza. A contemporary named Bepeshes, who was also a prince of Libyan descent, was buried in a small room north of the temple of Isis, in a poor wooden sarcophagus now in the Museum of Fine Arts in Boston; a beautiful bronze statue of him was discovered at Memphis. There was thus a certain continuity in the occupation of these places, even in the most troubled times.

Objects from the Saite Period also have been found at Giza. A small limestone sphinx about 8 inches in length was discovered near the temenos of the Sphinx. Its body is painted red with a checkerboard motif:

black lines enclosing red and yellow squares form a mantle on its back. It was dedicated to Harmakhis, "who grants life," by an individual named Hor, son of Hor. It is securely dated by the cartouche of Apries on its right shoulder. However humble the piece and however mediocre its craftsmanship, it has the merit of testifying to the continuity of the devotion paid to the Sphinx. Figurines were constantly dedicated to it, though many of those that have been found are not inscribed. This one supplies a precise chronological guidepost, the reign of King Apries of Dynasty 26, a period that saw a great deal of activity, including the restoration of monuments and cults. This era has often been called the Saite renaissance, for it was characterized by a taste for archaism and a search for old forms not only in relief and sculpture in the round but also in language and bureaucratic titles that had fallen into disuse. Despite the sometimes negative judgments that have been passed on this period, however, it never indulged in slavish imitation. Egyptians of that era were able to unite the past with "modern" elements, especially in the evolution of religious beliefs. A modicum of attention makes it impossible to confuse a Saite work of art with its Old or Middle Kingdom model.

THE STELA OF THE DAUGHTER OF CHEOPS

The objects from this period are not particularly informative, and their origins are sometimes uncertain. One, however, permits us to characterize the actual state of affairs under Dynasty 26. This is the so-called Stela of the Daughter of Cheops (Figure 15), also known as the Inventory Stela, which was found by Mariette in 1858 and taken to the museum in Cairo. A certain imprecision hovers over its discovery. It was found in the temple of Isis, but the excavator did not specify whether it was set into a wall, which must have been its original location, or whether it had already been dislodged. The stela is about 30 inches high and 15 inches wide, made of a hard limestone that is difficult to carve. At first glance, the stela seems scarcely worth looking at and could go unnoticed in the corner where it has been placed in a room dedicated to the Old Kingdom because of the presence of the name of Cheops. But its systematic analysis, especially if we confront the serious difficulties caused by lacunae and weathering in the last part of the text, enables us to discover the mine of

Figure 15. Stela of the Daughter of Cheops. Cairo Museum, JE 2091. Grdseloff MSS 1.19.1. © Griffith Institute, Oxford.

information it contains, on the historical level as well as the geographical and the religious.

The stela is rectangular and divided into four registers. It is covered with representations of deities, accompanied by legends of varying lengths, all of which are surrounded by a projecting frame. The frame bears a double text that is carved horizontally and vertically. It is carved in a block, the front part of which forms a horizontal edge upon which the text was continued, for the vertical part did not offer enough room. To understand the interest of this document, whose content has inspired more than one commentary, it is necessary to turn to the texts and draw out all the information they furnish. The inscription on the frame concisely states the project that was commemorated by the erection of this stela:

> Live the Horus Medjed, the King of Upper and Lower Egypt, Cheops, given life. He found the house of Isis, Mistress of the Pyramids, next to the house of Haurun, northwest of the house of Osiris, Lord of Rasetau. He (re)built the pyramid of the king's daughter Henutsen beside this temple. He made an inventory, carved on a stela, for his mother Isis, the mother of the god, Hathor, Mistress of the Sky. He restored for her the divine offerings and (re)built her temple in stone, that which he found in ruins being renewed, and the gods in their place.

The last statement is illustrated by the representations in the four registers. They are images of divine statues, and for the most part, there is a specification of the material they are made of and their size. In the first register, we see Min, then standards supporting figures of Wepwawet in the form of a jackal, Horus the falcon, and Thoth in his ibis form. The second register is dedicated essentially to Isis: first, there is the image of her barque, called "Support of the Splendor of Isis";[2] then we see Isis the Great, Mother of the God, Mistress of the Pyramids; Hathor in her

---

[2] Egyptian deities had portable sacred barques that the priests lifted and carried with the help of poles during processions outside the temples.

barque;[3] Nephthys, who was the sister of Isis and traditionally associated with her; Isis-Meskhenet, a syncretism associating Isis with the goddess who presided over childbirth; and finally, Isis in the form of a scorpion. The third register contains members of the family of Osiris, along with deities of Memphis: Harendotes and Harpokrates, aspects of Horus as avenger of his father and as a child; Ptah and Sakhmet; Osiris; Isis "who is on the throne"; Isis of the mammisi (birth house); and finally a child god whose name is illegible. The bottom register is occupied by the Apis bull; the emblem of Nefertem; a human-headed serpent goddess personifying the uraeus, or perhaps a local Renenutet; and a beautiful representation of the statue of Harmakhis in its usual form, a recumbent sphinx wearing a *nemes*, its chin adorned with a curved beard, on a tall pedestal with a cavetto cornice. In front of the sphinx are five columns of text divided in two by an empty column that immediately draws our attention to a rare detail in the organization of the inscription. The sculptor, who did not have enough space on the vertical surface for all of the long text dedicated to the Sphinx, carved the beginning of it in the first columns, continued it with four horizontal lines, which are difficult to read, on the upper surface of the base, and then finished it with the two vertical columns just in front of the Sphinx, which are separated from the preceding ones by the empty column. This part of the text is thus not to be read continuously, for it represents only the beginning and the end of the inscription, a fact that is also stressed by the repetition of the last words of each section of the text, a clever but unusual procedure. The length of the text illustrates that the Sphinx plays a major role in this document. Although part of the text is unclear, because of problems with reading the hieroglyphs and the many lacunae, the text contains a great deal of valuable information:

The temenos of Haurun-Harmakhis is south of the temple domain of Isis, Mistress of the Pyramids, and north of Osiris, Lord of Rasetau. The writings of the temple of Harmakhis were brought to make the inventory (*bis*) of this divine being (?) of the great [. . .] his effigy, its casing entirely covered with designs [. . .] he made [. . .] which is in gilded

---

[3] In this period, there was a close association of Isis, the mother goddess par excellence, with Hathor, goddess of pleasure and love.

stone of seven cubits [. . .] in the temenos of Harmakhis, in conformity with this model that is carved [. . .]. He set up an offering table for the vases [. . .]. May he endure. May he live forever and ever, his face turned toward the east.

These figures and their legends are added to the commemorative text carved on the frame, and unless we find the connecting thread that enables us to explain them, they can seem puzzling. A first point catches our attention, if only because of its rarity: the titulary of Cheops. The style of the piece and the deities chosen for representation illustrate that the stela could not be an Old Kingdom original, as certain scholars attempted to affirm just after it was discovered.[4] There was also talk of a copy of an authentic text of that early period, piously reproduced by distant successors. This is a practice we occasionally encounter in Egypt, but in such cases, the writers took care to indicate it. It is also necessary to exercise caution with regard to such replicas of an original document, for when a model actually existed, it was usually rewritten and recast to the taste of the day. But we find nothing of that sort in this case. There is only the name of Cheops, and the constructions that are mentioned are attributed to him. After renouncing the fabricated authenticity of the document, scholars went to the opposite extreme, calling it an ostensibly false work intended to misrepresent reality and to deceive those who could read it. Of the innumerable monuments bearing a royal name, some of those attributed to monarchs of the Old Kingdom are related to our stela. An example is the "Famine Stela" carved on a rock wall on the island of Sehel in the name of Djoser, a pharaoh of Dynasty 3, but in reality written in the Ptolemaic Period. Similarly, there are the inscriptions of the small Dynasty 18 temple at Medinet Habu, which were written in the reign of Hakoris of Dynasty 29 but bear the name of Tuthmosis III. But to employ terms like falsification and doctoring is to plaster a modern notion onto a concept of history entirely different from ours. The Egyptians also had a sense of history, but from a perspective far removed from our own. In using the name

---

[4] This misdating led to chronological aberrations, especially when "construct," rather than "reconstruct" was understood. The temple of Isis would have been older than the pyramids themselves!

of Cheops on this monument, the Egyptians were not attempting to attribute it to him, but rather to commemorate him, to recall his memory at the site where he built his funerary complex.

This context leads us to date the stela to the Saite Period, specifically to the beginning of Dynasty 26, which has left other traces. At that time a restoration effort was undertaken throughout the site, with the aim of reestablishing its glory. A new wooden sarcophagus with the name of Mycerinus was placed in his pyramid. The cults of the ancient kings were once again honored. The temple of Isis, which had been in regular use since Dynasty 21, was restored and enlarged, and the Sphinx was also repaired. The picture is coherent. Are we to attribute this work to a pharaoh—Psammetichus I, for example—under whom various enterprises were carried out? This is possible, but it cannot be maintained as certain. Someone with sufficient influence, who was well acquainted with the local cults, could have undertaken this restoration at his own expense. The consecration text on the stela evokes what were undoubtedly renovations, not new constructions: renovations of the pyramids of Cheops and the royal daughter Henutsen, and of the temple of Isis itself.

As for the Great Pyramids, excavations have not revealed traces of such repairs, though the interiors were badly disturbed in antiquity and the exteriors were ultimately used as quarries. Henutsen, a name attested in the Old Kingdom, appears in no document of the Saite Period in connection with a member of the royal family. Was the name reinvented from scratch at this time to conform with the Old Kingdom coloration of the stela? The repairs to the temple of Isis, which were accompanied by an inventory of its possessions, principally the divine statues kept in it, and by a renewal of the offerings dedicated to it, agree completely with both the *topos* of this genre of documents and with the archaeological record that has been recovered. The interesting part of this brief text is the topographical description, which situates the cult places with precision: the temple of Isis is near that of Haurun, which must have been linked to it by a road climbing the slope that separated them, and northwest of the temple of Osiris of Rasetau. The same indications are repeated in reverse order in the description of the temenos of Haurun-Harmakhis, which lay south of the temple of Isis and north of that of Osiris. Thus is depicted the landscape of Giza in Dynasty 26: the temple of Isis at the foot of the pyramid of Cheops, the Sphinx below it, and farther to the southwest, where the cultivation met the desert, the temple of Osiris. The text, which centers on the temple of Isis, indicates the close bonds that would dominate the three cult places from this time on. The lengthy description of the Sphinx is the proof of it; the description also proves that the cult of the Sphinx was indeed alive and that the monument was not neglected.

The statues that were the object of the inventory are represented in the central panel of the stela. The order of these twenty-two anthropomorphic or theriomorphic deities and divine emblems has been carefully arranged around the central figure of Isis. The order in which they are to be viewed is obvious, from right to left and from top to bottom. They are organized according to their order in religious processions, beginning with the various standards that preceded the barque of Isis, and then the images of specific forms of the goddess, who in that period was assuming the characteristics of a universal deity. She is accompanied by Osiris and by various forms of their son Horus. The most important deities of Memphis are also present: Ptah, Sakhmet, Nefertem, and the Apis bull. The inventory concludes with the statue of Harmakhis, also called Haurun-Harmakhis,[5] which is accompanied by an especially long legend that specifies its topographical coordinates. The archives of the temple of Harmakhis were consulted for the purpose of repairing damaged parts of the colossus, which was apparently decorated with painted elements. Some scholars have suggested that the stone that was replaced might have corresponded to the back of the *nemes*, but the text is in too bad a condition for that to be certain. There is also a question of meat offerings that were sacrificed to the god and consumed in his presence. The text concludes with a wish for eternity, while a final formula insists on his position facing east. Though many points in the text remain obscure, it appears that the cult of Haurun-Harmakhis continued to function according to established regulations, and that his temple possessed archives that were examined in order to repair his statue. Archaeological analysis of the colossus has shown that the second phase of restoration probably dated to the Saite Period, though few of these repairs have survived. The repairs were effected with large

---

[5] In this period, Haurun, who was originally a Syro-Palestinian god, was no longer viewed as foreign, and his name merely reflected a distant and assimilated past.

blocks of Tura limestone displaying tool marks, which are still visible, similar to those found on contemporary monuments such as the tomb of Tjary in the south of Giza. The content of the document, which is quite rich and original despite its mediocre appearance, reveals that the overseers of the restorations worked simultaneously at the temple of Isis and in the temenos of Harmakhis. They made a complete inventory of the cult places, repairing both of them and renewing the offering donations, while commemorating the name of Cheops, the first of the pharaohs who chose the plateau of Giza for their pyramids.

THE CHAPEL OF HARBES AND THE PRIESTHOODS OF HARMAKHIS

The temple of Isis consists of a complex ensemble of chapels built at different times around a nucleus, evidently with no preconceived plan. Some of these chapels have shafts leading to funerary chambers; these were pillaged long ago and have yielded little material. This practice of constructing tombs in a temenos, in the proximity of a temple, did not begin until Dynasty 21; the prototype was at Tanis, where royal tombs were located within the perimeter delimited by the enclosure wall built by Psusennes. We find the same phenomenon on a smaller scale at Giza, in the sector of the temple of Isis and in the immediate surroundings of the Sphinx. Such tombs continued to be constructed at Giza until the Ptolemaic Period.

Among the chapels built near the temple of Isis, one of them, in the northern part of the temenos, claims our attention for several reasons. Notwithstanding the damage wrought by time and human pillaging, we know its owner: Harbes, who had various court titles, including "chief of secrets" and "royal butler." He lived and worked under Psammetichus I, as attested by the presence of this king's cartouches on a number of his monuments, but his tomb has not been found. The partially preserved decoration of his chapel offers scenes that were common in temples: depictions of Isis, Osiris, and Nephthys. But we can assemble a rich dossier regarding this individual because of other evidence: several statues of stone or bronze, another bearing the name of his mother, a donation stela, undoubtedly in favor of the temple of Osiris of Rasetau, and an offering table. These objects were discovered at various times, some of them long ago, and they are scattered in museums throughout the world. One of them is connected with the cult of Harmakhis: it was discovered east of the temenos of the Sphinx, and not in Harbes' chapel. It is a limestone statue of a falcon, now headless, nearly 30 inches long and more than 20 inches high. It differs from other known representations of Harmakhis/Horus in that the bird is not standing upright, but rather is crouching, like the representations of mummified falcons or of the god Sokar. The base, which seems to be unfinished, includes two brief texts on the front and back. One text contains a title and the name of Harbes, along with that of his father, and the other the cartouche of Psammetichus, "beloved of Osiris, Horus, and Isis." This brief epithet summarizes the theology of Giza in this period. Osiris (of Rasetau) is named, and the mummified appearance of the falcon might be a metaphorical allusion to the god's Sokar aspect. But this same falcon could also evoke Horus, and indirectly Harmakhis, though the latter is not specifically mentioned. Isis completes the triad. The documents at our disposal indicate that this dignitary, who must have been wealthy to judge from the number of his monuments, privileged Isis and Osiris, but he did not neglect the Sphinx, which was between the temples of the two deities.

The chapel of Harbes offers equally valuable information regarding the cults that flourished in this period. After Harbes decorated the room, a family of priests added carvings of their own on the northern and eastern walls, though they respected the existing reliefs and in some cases imitated them. They added a number of graffiti, which are difficult to read but open new perspectives. There is a total of fifteen such texts, two of which were cut out of the wall and taken to the museum in Cairo in the nineteenth century. The rest of the graffiti, which are still *in situ*, have deteriorated over the years, because of inconsiderate visitors who have scribbled on top of them.

Collecting the information scattered throughout these inscriptions, scholars have reconstructed the family tree of these priests through six generations; the last member of this family appears only on a stela at the Serapeum and on a sumptuous gold ring that probably came from Giza. The stela furnishes a precise date, year 34 of Darius, which enables us to place the known ancestor of the family in the time of Psammetichus I; the last of its members lived at the end of the reign of Darius and in that of Xerxes, during the first Persian domination of Egypt. Pami, the earliest known member of the family, could have been a contemporary of Harbes, but we have no indication of either a family tie between the two men or of any relationship between the offices they held. The carving of the graffiti evidently began later, in the third generation, during the reign of Amasis; most of the texts date from the reign of Darius. All the members of the family[6] have religious titles, organized in series that are for the most part quite similar to one another. One series attaches some of these individuals to the temple of Ptah in Memphis, where they were prophets, *wab* (pure) priests, and masters of secrets. Another series seems to be more specifically linked to Giza, with mention of masters of secrets of Rasetau. The holders of this office also had titles of a funerary nature, describing them as specialists who carried out offerings, libations, and censings.[7]

More remarkable is the series of titles, which recurs with only slight variations, borne by one member of each generation except the fourth; each man transmitted it to his son and heir. Pami, Pasherieniset I and II, Psammetichus, and Psammetichus-men-em-Pe each held the titles prophet of Isis, Mistress of the Pyramids; god's father and prophet of Harmakhis; prophet of the King of Upper and Lower Egypt Cheops; prophet of Chephren; and president of the necropolis. Their titles also sometimes included prophet of Harendotes, Lord of Rasetau, and prophet of Mycerinus and Radjedef. It seems natural that these people were also priests of Isis, for they carved their genealogy in her very temple. What is more unusual is that they included the title of prophet of Harmakhis; if this title existed before their time, it remains unknown to us. This fact stresses the close relationship that would thenceforth exist among the major sites on the Giza plateau.

[6] These genealogies are strictly masculine; only the names of the individuals' mothers are mentioned. In this context, it is quite surprising that none of the women was a priestess or songstress of Isis, and that their names do not reveal any special devotion to that goddess, as is the case with a certain number of the men in the family.

[7] Osiris, Lord of Rasetau, is not explicitly present in these texts, though the holders of priestly titles held offices in the cemeteries. It would seem that the priests of Osiris were separate from those of Isis, Harmakhis, and the kings, and that their offices were entrusted to different persons.

At the same time, we witness the reappearance of priesthoods of ancient kings, especially Cheops and Chephren, which were directly connected with the temple of Isis and the temenos of Harmakhis, and more sporadically of Mycerinus and Radjedef, the last of whom was buried farther north, at Abu Rawash. These offices were borrowed from the titularies of officials of the Old Kingdom, where they occurred in great number. The surrounding mastabas were entered in this later period, if only for reuse in secondary burials. The significance we accord these titles is of course different from their meaning at the time of their creation. Their holders were not literally funerary priests of these kings, assuring their worship and the dedication of offerings to them; their funerary cults had long since been abandoned, never to be reestablished. These titles were a way of honoring the names of these somewhat forgotten sovereigns, commemorating them alongside the deities Isis and Harmakhis. These priestly offices have often been called fictive, which conjures up an unjustifiably negative connotation. Even if these cults remained local, as was often the case in Egypt, they testify to a genuine desire to bring the past back to life via worship that joined these kings to the deities who were revered at the time. This situation is comparable to the one that caused the erection of the Stela of the Daughter of Cheops, and it clearly shows that there was no official condemnation of the memory of the kings who built the Dynasty 4 pyramids, as claimed by Herodotus (*Histories*, II, 128). Cheops, the perverse king who prostituted his daughter, and his successor Chephren supposedly closed the temples and cast the Egyptians into profound misery: "In their hatred for these kings, the Egyptians absolutely refuse to utter their names, and they even call the pyramids by the name of Philitis, a shepherd who at that time pastured his flocks nearby." The Greek historian probably lent an ear to stories and legends, some of them drawn from Egyptian literature. The stories from Papyrus Westcar contrast the tyrannical Cheops with the pious Snofru, casting discredit on the former. But otherwise, their names lived on in ancient inscriptions discovered at Giza and in the king lists that constitute official sources. In this phenomenon, we see a deliberate effort that was characteristic of the times, even if its scope was limited to Giza. Under the aegis of the Mistress of the Pyramids, the founders of the great royal cemetery with the figure of Harmakhis at its center were commemorated. The aura of antiquity radiated over the entire site, the continued life of which was marked by innumerable construction works, observance of the cults, and visits of pilgrims.

HARMAKHIS AND HIS TEMENOS
DURING THE LAST DYNASTIES

The objects dedicated to Harmakhis during Dynasty 26 and later are not very numerous. Furthermore, they often cannot be exactly dated, which makes attributing them to a precise period difficult. Many votive sphinxes were dedicated to Harmakhis, including those in the museums in Boston, Cairo, and London. Certain stelae might also be attributable to this period. A small limestone base that once supported a disappeared statue is dedicated to the specific form of Harmakhis-Shu, father of Re, and to a local god of the Faiyum, Mestasymtis, "Hearing Ears"; it is the only mention of the latter outside his own domain. Perhaps this piece is to be attributed to pilgrims from the Faiyum who made a connection between two gods: the personification of the ears that hear, once represented as a face viewed full front, and the face of the Sphinx, which was also known to be attentive to prayers and sometimes also depicted accompanied by ears. In the chapel of Haurun-Harmakhis, a stela-naos bearing the name of Petiese, evidently from Dynasty 26, was discovered behind the stela of Amenophis II. Petiese is depicted in the round in the niche, in adoration before Osiris and Isis. Assuming that the object is not intrusive, it suggests that in this period, objects not devoted to the Sphinx itself could be deposited in this chapel.

There was a new phenomenon that first appeared in Dynasty 26 and continued down to the Hellenistic Period in both Egyptian and Greek names. Surprisingly, although the cult of Harmakhis flourished during Dynasties 18 and 19, there were no personal names that contained the name of the god or simply repeated it. It is often a criterion of the popularity of a deity that he or she was honored in this manner or that people employed the deity's name to place a child under his or her protection. This absence is perhaps explained by the fact that the cult of the Sphinx did not develop in an urban center, but rather in the desert, so that worshipers had to make a special visit to the plateau of Giza. Curiously, beginning with Dynasty 26, we find some persons bearing the name of Harmakhis, especially at Giza: a stela dating probably to the Saite Period, found near the tomb of Tjary, was dedicated by a certain Harmakhis, son of Petiese, to Osiris, Lord of Rasetau. Canopic jars testifying to a burial in the cemetery east of the pyramid of Cheops belonged to Harmakhis, son of Hedebiru. From the same area at Giza, we have a group of 324 *ushabtis* (funerary figurines) that were made for yet another Harmakhis, son of Hotep-Bastet-iru. A tomb north of the causeway of Chephren has furnished a *ushabti* of still another bearer of this name. Since much of the funerary material of this era has disappeared, nothing prevents us from thinking that this name was even more widespread, though we have no indication as to why it became fashionable at this time. The name also found takers outside Giza. Further canopic jars bearing this name have been found at Saqqara, and during the Ptolemaic Period a high priest of Ptah and prophet of the deified Queen Arsinoe had the name Harmakhis. The name was also adopted by Greeks, and it appears in lists of persons who lived in villages in the delta. But with this passage into a community that spoke a different language, the reasons for choosing the name could have been different from those of native Egyptians.

We must consider one last aspect of the temenos of Harmakhis and its surroundings, which were protected by new brick walls that replaced those erected by Tuthmosis IV. During the New Kingdom, there was little or no use of the Giza plateau as a cemetery. At that time, religious activities related to the world of the living replaced the funerary purpose that had motivated the pharaohs of Dynasty 4 to choose the site. During the Third Intermediate Period, when the chapel of Isis was enlarged, people were once again buried there such as the Libyan named Bepeshes noted earlier. But the heyday of Giza's reuse as a cemetery was from Dynasty 26 through the Ptolemaic Period. In varying degrees, this phenomenon affected the entire plateau: burials in the temenos of the temple of Isis; reuse of ancient mastabas, with the digging of new burial shafts; makeshift graves in the eastern cemetery and near the tomb of Queen Khentkaus; creation of a vast cemetery, today in devastated condition, south of the rocky spur that dominates the site, and whose most beautiful tomb, with archaizing reliefs, belonged to Tjary, a high official and priest of Krokodilopolis in the Faiyum; and finally, tombs in immediate proximity to the Sphinx. As early as the Old Kingdom, rock-cut tombs had been excavated on the side of the slope leading up from the depression of the Sphinx toward the eastern cemetery. Some of them, today inaccessible, had been reused during the New Kingdom in the framework of the cult of Harmakhis; in the first millennium, they were perhaps already covered with sand and no longer utilized.

Northwest of the Sphinx, four tombs were excavated in the rocky border that delimited the upper part of the temenos, the terrace where the chapel of Harmakhis had been erected. We have no means of affirming that they existed in the Old Kingdom and were simply reused in the Late Period. When they were discovered, two of them were decorated, but the decoration has disappeared; the unpublished notes of John Wilkinson are our only source of information regarding them. The oldest, going back to Dynasty 26, belonged to a certain Ptahirdis; its two-columned forecourt undoubtedly reproduced an Old Kingdom model somewhere in the vicinity. Just to the south is that of Petubastis, whose façade was covered with representations of Osiris and the deceased, and with texts including the titles of this person, who held high civil and military offices. He was originally from the city of Leontopolis, where he had ties with the temple of the god Mahes. Various indications, particularly the details of the clothing, lead us to think that this dignitary lived around Dynasty 30 or the beginning of the Ptolemaic Period. Nothing in the titles of these men indicates a special tie to Harmakhis, though it was undoubtedly their desire to be near this god that motivated them to choose this location for their tombs.

A little farther away—north of the causeway of Chephren, which was probably in bad condition in this period, and west of the temenos of the Sphinx—the Saite Period saw the excavation of a series of tombs in a previously unoccupied area. Some of the tombs had a superstructure and consisted of a single room with a shaft cut into the rock, and some of these rooms were decorated. They had already been plundered when Howard Vyse and Patrick Campbell discovered them in the nineteenth century. Today, they are in highly damaged condition and cannot be entered, and no systematic plans have ever been made of them. A simple pit sheltered the sarcophagi of General Amasis, son of the king of the same name, and his mother, Nakhtbastetiru, the king's wife; they might have been transferred to Giza after being buried elsewhere, in order to preserve them. Campbell's Tomb, named after its discoverer, consists of a huge pit with the actual vault constructed at its bottom; an extremely deep trench circled the pit at some distance from it. This system, which was peculiar to the period, was supposed to make it possible, after the burial was completed, to fill everything with sand and thus prevent plundering, though success was not always assured. The tomb excavated for Pakap also sheltered the sarcophagus of Ptahhotep, a dignitary of the Persian Period, and those of two notables originally from Imet in the east delta, both of them named Nesisut, who probably lived during Dynasty 30. In this case as well, high-ranking persons from somewhat distant places who held offices in the administration of Memphis chose to be buried in a prestigious location near the Great Pyramids and the Sphinx.

During this period, which was filled with ups and downs but far from on the decline, the Sphinx continued to be venerated as a god named Haurun-Harmakhis. The colossus was restored when the repairs made during Dynasty 18 began to show signs of dilapidation. The most original aspect of this period rests in the transformations experienced by the cult of the Sphinx. During the New Kingdom, the environs of the statue had been brought back to life at the initiative of kings who placed themselves under the Sphinx's protection. The first millennium saw the increasing influence of deities who had previously had a low profile, in the context of the religious evolution of the time. In her little chapel, an Old Kingdom building that was transformed and redeployed for new purposes, Isis assumed the role of Mistress of the Pyramids, while signs increasingly indicated the veneration of Osiris of Rasetau. As attested by the Stela of the Daughter of Cheops, the local priests set out to create ties between these three places and these three deities: Harmakhis implicitly represented Horus, son of Isis and Osiris. At the same time, the memory of ancient kings was revived, and the site gained increasing prestige, laden with a history that had never been obscured. The Late Period mixed the old and the new, while the Sphinx, according to the Egyptian text, kept his gaze fixed eternally eastward.

7

The Greco-Roman Period

Radical changes affected Egypt after the end of the native dynasties and the arrival of Alexander the Great, but its religious life remained no less lively. The new pharaohs—Greeks, then Romans—mostly proved desirous of safeguarding and embellishing existing monuments, and they promulgated or approved policies of fresh construction. Egypt was filled with new temples, a few of which are preserved in their entirety, while scores of others have been reduced to portions of walls or columns—or even just to a few blocks. Egyptian culture did not shed its own characteristics because of these new arrivals, who adopted native cults or created mixed deities such as Sarapis, whose cult was promoted with remarkable success. The new arrivals sometimes honored Egyptian deities in their Greek manner, equating their gods and goddesses with those of Egypt, and even comparing Greek and Egyptian phenomena. This is what happened in the Greek texts dedicated to the Sphinx, which reveal that the two cultures did not live in ignorance of each other, but rather that exchanges took place, based on a degree of mutual understanding and acceptance.

Before turning to the changes that took place in the appearance of the site, beginning at a time that cannot easily be determined, we should consider the unique literary and historical testimony that has been handed down to us. Herodotus saw all the activity that surrounded the Sphinx but remained silent regarding it. Diodorus (*Library of History*, I, 63.2–64) and

Strabo (*Geography*, XVII, 1.33–34) were equally silent; the former wrote in the middle of the first century B.C.E., and the latter visited Egypt just after it passed under Roman domination. Both evoke the plateau of the Great Pyramids, which they list among the Seven Wonders of the World, but without taking note of the Sphinx. It is not until Pliny the Elder, who perished in the eruption of Mount Vesuvius in 79 C.E., that we finally find mention of the Sphinx in classical literature. His *Natural History*, composed of thirty-seven books, is a vast compilation that reads like a stack of note cards, and Pliny indicates that he consulted two thousand works in drawing his material together. In the course of this treatment of a vast number of topics, he surveys various constructions, including the pyramids of Giza (XXXVII, 12):

> In Egypt too are the pyramids, which must be mentioned, if only cursorily. They rank as a superfluous and foolish display of wealth on the part of the kings, since it is generally recorded that their motive for building them was to avoid providing funds for their successors or for rivals who wished to plot against them, or else to keep the common folk occupied. Much vanity was shown by these kings in regard to such enterprises, and the remains of several unfinished pyramids are still in existence. . . . The other three pyramids, the fame of which has reached every part of the world, are of course visible to travellers approaching by river from any direction. They stand on a rocky hill in the desert on the African side of the river between the city of Memphis and what, as we have already explained, is known as the Delta, at a point less than 4 miles from the Nile, and 7½ miles from Memphis. Close by is a village called Busiris, where there are people who are used to climbing these pyramids.
>
> In front of them is the Sphinx, which deserves to be described even more than they, and yet the Egyptians have passed over it in silence. The inhabitants of the region regard it as a deity. They are of the opinion that a King Harmais is buried inside it and try to make out that it was brought to the spot: it is in fact carefully fashioned from the native rock. The face of the monstrous creature is painted with a ruddle as a sign of reverence. The circumference of the head when measured across the forehead amounts to 102 feet, the length is 243 feet, and the height from the paunch to the top of the asp on its head is 61½ feet. . . . and the last and greatest

of these wonders, which forbids us to marvel at the wealth of kings, is that the smallest but most greatly admired of these pyramids was built by Rhodopis, a mere prostitute. She was once the concubine of Aesop, the sage who composed the Fables; and our amazement is all the greater when we reflect that such wealth was acquired through prostitution.

Pliny's observations on pyramids in general and those of Giza in particular offer no new information. Like his predecessors, he is torn between admiration inspired by the size of these monuments, which had no equal in ancient Greece, and criticism of the vanity of these works, for which their tyrannical builders ruined their land and enslaved their people. This perception is foreign to the goals pursued by the Egyptians of the Old Kingdom, of which the Greeks and Romans certainly had no idea. Their sense of an ideal led them to other concepts of public buildings, concepts related to the ideal of city or empire.

Pliny's mention of Busiris evidently is a reference to the Letopolite Busiris, named in the Greek texts in honor of the Sphinx, and not the Busiris that was a little farther south in the direction of Saqqara. Moreover, we know that when Egyptian names passed into the Greek language, the name of the towns called Busiris, which were legion, concealed the phrase *per Usir*, "house of Osiris." Such allusions to the temple of Osiris, Lord of Rasetau (with the latter epithet fallen away), appear in numerous Egyptian sources. Busiris already existed in the Ramesside Period, when the text on a donation stela designated it the "village of Rasetau." We thus know that the site was in continuous existence from the New Kingdom until Roman times; although it was not a large place, it benefited from the celebrity of the Great Pyramids and the Sphinx, for pilgrims and tourists were obliged to pass through it.

In this final period of activity, we find two factors converging: a religious goal, along with secular intentions that can be called the first instance of tourism, in which many Greeks and Romans participated. The inhabitants of the village were already climbing the pyramids. Pliny's phrase is laconic, and we are left to imagine that this activity was intended to entertain the tourists; or perhaps, like the dragomen of the nineteenth century, the climbers charged a fee to assist those who were unable to make their own way up these mountains of stone. The anecdote raises a more serious issue. If scaling the pyramids was already fashionable in the first century of our own era, it was because, in part at least, they no longer possessed their smooth casing slabs of granite, like those still to be seen at the top of Chephren's pyramid; otherwise, the activity would have been especially dangerous. In the Middle Kingdom, the only period when the site was abandoned, pharaohs helped themselves to blocks that they reused in other constructions, without considering this to be an act of pillage. The practice continued in the New Kingdom, when older buildings were demolished to construct new ones in their place. It is thus not particularly surprising that the casings of the pyramids were no longer intact in the Roman Period. We cannot, however, determine how much of them had been lost. This practice continued during the Middle Ages, as reported by the earliest Western travelers. The Giza plateau was the most convenient quarry for the builders of Cairo to exploit.

Pliny furnishes a brief but admiring description of the Sphinx; in the Latin text, the word "sphinx" is feminine in gender, a simple transposition of the gender of the Greek word. He calls the "monstrous creature" a local deity without giving its Greek name Harmakhis, which is known otherwise from contemporary documents. In addition to some measurements—length, height, circumference of the head—he notes the red color of the face; faint traces are still visible, but the color must have been more vivid in Pliny's day. The most valuable information—and today the most obvious, though it would not have been self-evident in antiquity—is that the colossus is carved from the native rock. Pliny stresses that certain people claimed that the monument had been brought to the place it occupied. Though his sentence is not very clear, it leads us to think that sources unknown to us treated the Sphinx as a statue like any other, which would have been sculpted and then placed there to serve a particular function. Again according to the statements he reports, the statue was actually the tomb of a king named Harmais. We do not know the origin of this fantastic legend, but it had a long life, for even in Maspero's day, subterranean chambers were imagined to lie underneath the Sphinx. Not until the last decades of the twentieth century did electromagnetic resistivity testing on the surfaces of the statue put an end to these allegations, which were always ready to resurface.

How are we to explain the birth of such traditions about a tomb? We do not find them mentioned elsewhere in classical literature or in epigraphic texts of the same period, much less in the Egyptian documentation. A plausible answer would be to see them as a displacement due to proximity, with the pyramids' function as royal tombs being transferred to the Sphinx. Describing the Great Pyramids and the hatred their builders supposedly attracted to themselves, Diodorus follows the tradition of Herodotus; he adds, however, that the pharaohs were never buried in them, but rather that the rulers commanded that their bodies be placed in a secure place that was kept secret. This statement could also explain the sepulchral role unexpectedly attributed to the Sphinx. Who was Harmais? Certain scholars have wished to identify him with Harmakhis, the name of the Sphinx from the New Kingdom on, who from being a god would have become a king again. Unfortunately, phonetics make this explanation highly unsatisfying, for there is no good reason for the letter *chi* ("kh") to have been lost from the name, given that at that time, the Greeks were correctly rendering Har-em-akhet as Harmakhis. Yet we also find the name in Diodorus, who presents in turn two traditions regarding the pharaohs who built the pyramids. One of them, the more common tradition, mentions Cheops, Chephren, and Mycerinus, just as in Herodotus. But, adds Diodorus,

> there is lack of unanimity concerning these pyramids, both among the natives of the place and among historians. Some say the above-mentioned kings erected them. But some say it was certain others: for example, some claim that Armaeus made the largest one, Amosis the second, and Inaros the third; and some people assert that this last is the burial place of Rhodopis the courtesan, of whom they relate that certain of the nomarchs, who were her lovers, built the structure in common out of affection for her.

Like Herodotus before him, our author used several contradictory sources without discriminating among them or subjecting them to critical analysis. Examination of the texts of the Greek historians reveals a certain confusion between the sovereigns of Dynasty 4 and those of Dynasty 26, as is the case with the names of Amosis (Amasis) and Inaros. The first individual, Armaeus (Armais), is undoubtedly the same ruler mentioned by Pliny. The name, which is well attested in Greek, has been identified with Egyptian Haremhab, "Horus is in festival," which was borne by the last king of Dynasty 18. We also find the name in this form in Manetho's list of kings. But there is scarcely any reason for the construction of the Great Pyramid or the Sphinx to have been attributed to this pharaoh, and if there was a tradition, even an erroneous one, concerning all three pyramids, we could expect it to be consistent and to evoke only persons, royal or otherwise, from the Saite Period. The legend of the courtesan Rhodophis, who funded the building of the third pyramid with donations from her lovers, takes place in the same period. Harmais-Haremhab remains mysterious. He is also found—if the identification is correct—in other Egyptian contexts, where he is a local god or perhaps a deified saintly individual. The indications we have from Diodorus and Pliny are too indirect and confused for us to resolve the matter. They derive from the same source, which existed alongside more reliable documents concerning Egyptian history. Pliny, who displays no sign of critical acumen, nevertheless took pleasure in waxing ironic about the vanity of builders whose names he was not even sure of!

In this confusion of stories and legends, both Greek and Egyptian, which Pliny makes no effort to straighten out, one partial sentence calls for comment: ". . . the Sphinx . . . (the Egyptians) have passed it over in silence." (The passage cited is an interpretation on the part of the translator; Pliny's text says simply: ". . . about which *they* are silent.") This statement raises questions. Is the author simply stating, as we have done, that his predecessors omitted mention of the Sphinx, or does he mean that there were reasons that prevented its mention? When Herodotus felt he had to remain silent regarding certain information he had gathered in Egypt, such as details regarding Osiris, he justified his silence with the need to maintain secrecy. Should we seek a similar phenomenon with respect to the Sphinx? No argument supports such a hypothesis, especially given that this open-air colossus was the paragon of a deity who was intended to be seen. If we review the chronology from the sixth century on, Herodotus was certainly able to view the Sphinx cleared from the sands, for in his day, there was intense activity at the site. From their archaeological characteristics, the huge protective walls serving to hold back the sand date to Dynasty 30 or the beginning of the Ptolemaic Period. The upper levels that covered those of the New Kingdom in the "villa" built in front of Chephren's valley temple also date back to the Hellenistic era. These constructions testify that life went on around the Sphinx. Small objects, such as sphinxes and lions of various sizes, are also contemporary. Yet few Egyptian finds can be securely dated to the Ptolemaic Period. The Greek inscriptions that have been studied are later. Dated documents testifying to repairs or clearing in the area of the Sphinx are Roman. Are we to think that a period of relative abandonment occurred during the three centuries of Ptolemaic rule, and that it was only later, in Roman Egypt, that there was fresh interest in the colossus? The hypothesis cannot be excluded, at least if we set aside the temple of Osiris of Rasetau, for stelae were dedicated to this god during the Ptolemaic Period.

Beginning at a time that cannot be determined, major renovations were carried out regularly until the second century of our own era. The first modern excavators found the site in its final condition, and it remained the same until Baraize demolished the Roman constructions to reach the earlier levels. To describe the ultimate appearance of the site, it is thus necessary to rely on Caviglia's account and Salt's drawings, along with Baraize's photographs and notes. In the Roman period, and perhaps even in the Ptolemaic era, the Sphinx was approached from the east via a monumental entranceway that could have served only to impress visitors. Its orientation was the same as that of the access route that led to it. From an upper platform, visitors descended a double stairway with eleven steps that opened onto another large platform nearly 43 feet long by 40 feet wide. In the center of the first staircase rose a podium that Caviglia and Salt proposed to restore with two columns, on the basis of the architectural remains they found in place. This construction had disappeared by the time that Baraize resumed excavations in the area; only traces of its foundation remained. On the front of the podium, facing the Sphinx, was carved a lacuna-ridden inscription dating to 199–200, in the reign of Septimius Severus, who visited Egypt. The inscription alludes to renovations, and perhaps to a pavement. At the other end of the platform rose a second podium with the same orientation; it was approached by four steps and also had two columns. From there, a huge staircase with 30 steps nearly 40 feet wide descended, opening onto the temenos. To the north and the

south, walls of unbaked brick bordered this access route. These constructions towered more than 30 feet above the Sphinx, and they were built
over the roof of the so-called Sphinx temple.

From the bottom of the staircase to the forelegs of the Sphinx, the
ground was covered with limestone pavement (Figures 16 and 17); some
traces of it still remain, though they are in bad condition. A granite altar
was erected just in front of the forelegs. Its base is still *in situ*, while its
upper part, in the form of a "horned altar," is now in the British Museum.
Traces of fire remained in it; this type of altar, of which we have many examples, was generally used for burnt offerings. The ends of the forelegs
enclosed a chapel that was built between them. We do not know what
kind of cult was practiced in this chapel. It was an eclectic affair that was
largely made of earlier elements, such as the stelae of Tuthmosis IV and
Ramesses II, to which new portions were added in a different style. The
space was closed by two screen walls perpendicular to the forelegs, with
an entrance to the axis of the chapel. The front of the construction was
guarded by a rather crudely made lion that must have belonged to a pair.
The space between the forelegs was entirely paved with limestone and divided into two parts by two other low walls. All these elements, which
were again covered by the sands after the excavations of the nineteenth
century, were ultimately removed by Baraize. Though we cannot trace the
continuous evolution of the temenos of the Sphinx during the seven centuries that elapsed between the conquest of Alexander and the end of the
Roman domination, we nevertheless can estimate what happened. During the Ptolemaic Period, the site probably remained in more or less its
state at the end of Dynasty 30. The walls erected at that time continued to
protect it from the sands, at least for a while. Accounting for the surrounding structures is difficult, however; for example, we do not know
whether the chapel erected by Amenophis II was still in use. Excavation
has revealed no significant trace of Ptolemaic construction, but we cannot
assert that there was none. Constructions could have disappeared as early
as the Roman Period, or later, when the plateau was subject to wholesale
pillaging. The site incontestably profited during the Roman Empire.
Large-scale works were carried out at Giza during the first and second
centuries C.E., in conformity with the desire of some of the Roman
pharaohs to restore the major sites of ancient Egypt, and with their cu-

Figure 16. Detail of the forelegs of the Sphinx, with the stela of Tuthmosis IV in the background and the Roman paving in the foreground, 1925. Archives Lacau. Centre W. Golenischeff, EPHE, Vᵉ section.

riosity regarding a religion that seemed exotic to them. We must also consider the vigilance that the inhabitants of the neighborhood always manifested toward their monument. In a grandiose vision, the colossal statue of purely Egyptian style mingled with a series of Roman architectural elements that defined its access, replacing the constructions of the New Kingdom.

Tourists and the faithful continued to visit the Sphinx and to have simple dedications carved on one of its forelegs or on a limestone plaque. Some of the visitors wrote longer compositions that reflect the concepts that prevailed in those times. Securely dated texts allow us to fix the milestones in the various renovations that were carried out in the environs of the Sphinx. The first is a decree from the reign of Tiberius in 22–23 C.E., issued by the inhabitants of the village of Busiris in honor of the *strategos* (governor) of the Letopolite nome, Graecus Pompeius Sabinus. The text,

Figure 17. Detail of the area between the forelegs of the Sphinx, 1925. Archives Lacau. Centre W. Golenischeff, EPHE, V^e section.

inscribed on a stela that was found in front of the Sphinx, is fragmentary. It essentially concerns the good deeds of the *strategos*, for which the people of Busiris felt grateful. But the place selected for the public display of this decree—the temenos of the Sphinx—is revealing. During the reign of Nero, when Tiberius Claudius Balbillus was prefect of Egypt, the inhabitants of the same village commissioned the carving of another decree on a stela that was also set up near the Sphinx. That stela commemorates the clearing away of sand that must have invaded the area around the colossus. This prefect displayed a desire to restore the monuments of Egypt. He apparently traveled to the plateau of the Great Pyramids to venerate Helios-Harmakhis, the Egyptian god having been assimilated to the Greek sun god Helios. A third stela tells of the repair of the walls that surrounded the temenos in year 6 of the joint reign of Marcus Aurelius and Lucius Verus. In addition, the lower podium bears an inscription of Septimius Severus. Even if we assume that these works were for the most part not carried out at the instigation of the emperors themselves, they nevertheless denote a political will combined with curiosity and a religious interest in maintaining a prestigious monument, as was the case with the Colossi of Memnon.

At the same time, private people, evidently of Greek origin, were moved by a desire to commemorate their visits to the site. In addition to simple signatures, we also find texts, some of them poetic, that convey the sentiments of the visitors. Three of those texts are especially worthy of attention because of their descriptions of the Sphinx:

The walls of Thebes, which were raised by music, have also perished. But this wall, mine, escapes the cares of war and knows not the deeds of enemies, quite like moans. Without cease, feasts and shouting arouse joy, along with choruses of young men who assemble from all parts. It is flutes, not trumpets, that we hear, and the soil is wet with the blood of bulls, and not that of men who are killed.

Garments, not armor, are our finery, and our hand holds not a sword, but a cup, the companion of banquets. All night long, at the foot of the offerings that are ablaze, we celebrate Harmakhis, our heads covered with crowns, in our songs.

While not everything in this text is clear, there is nevertheless a definite contrast between Thebes in Greece with its sphinx and the temenos of Harmakhis, whose enclosure wall is perhaps evoked. Another contrast juxtaposes the ferocity of mortal combat and the joy of the festivities celebrated in the presence of Harmakhis. The second text relies on the same antithesis, adding further information that raises problems of interpretation:

> Your marvelous body was fashioned by the eternal gods in their care for the territory submitted to fire, and they placed it in the middle of a natural base, after having disposed of the sand from your rocky islet. This neighbor that they placed in sight of the pyramids is not, as at Thebes, the murderess of Oedipus, but the very holy servant of the goddess Leto, the guardian of the departed, beneficent Osiris, august guide of the land of Egypt, celestial [. . .] similar to Hephaestus [. . .] Arrian.

Aside from the comparison of the male and female sphinxes, which permits a stress on the beneficent character of the god, we find a sort of description of the Sphinx, which the Greeks considered to be the work of gods and not humans. The Sphinx is assigned the role of servant of Leto, the goddess who lent her name to the Letopolite nome, which was presided over by Horus, especially in his capacity of guardian of Osiris. The texts written in Egyptian offer no direct allusion to this concept of Harmakhis. Some scholars have connected this assertion with the supposed existence of a statue of Osiris resting against the right flank of the Sphinx, as described by Mariette. Or should we make a connection with the cult of Osiris of Rasetau, with the Sphinx having become, for the Greeks, the guardian of the site of Giza? From its epigraphy, the last of the inscriptions perhaps dates to the end of the second century; the ancient copy is to be treated with caution:

> He has a share of everything, this sphinx which is also a divine spectacle. In fact, if one beholds his body and its height, one notes all that makes the ornament of a very sacred prodigy. Above, he has a holy visage enlivened by divine breath, but he has the members and the stature of a lion, the king of beasts. A dreadful sight!

This example is remarkable for its precise description of the hybrid statue, with a lion's body and a man's head, which has become a god's head. The author of the epigram is gripped by fear before the spectacle of the composite god, who blends animality and sacredness to an abnormal degree. These inscriptions reveal that Greeks and Romans knew the myths and were more than merely curious visitors. It was a god whom they encountered in the person of the Sphinx, a sovereign god whom they connected with Helios, and a beneficent god, guardian of the plateau. The size of the monument, which still fascinates, filled them with respect and even fear. The myth of the Sphinx was born, and it would not cease to haunt the imagination of both the East and the West.

Bibliography

Chapter 1

A number of general studies on sphinxes can be consulted: U. Schweitzer, *Löwe und Sphinx im Alten Ägypten*, Ägyptologische Forschungen 15 (Glückstadt, 1948); C. de Wit, *Le Rôle et le sens du lion dans l'Égypte ancienne* (Leiden, 1951), esp. pp. 39–70; H. Demisch, *Die Sphinx: Geschichte ihrer Darstellung von den Anfängen bis zur Gegenwart* (Stuttgart, 1977); C. Zivie-Coche, *Lexikon der Ägyptologie*, vol. 5 (Wiesbaden, 1984), cols. 1139–47.

An interesting approach is taken by D. Meeks, "Zoomorphie et image des dieux dans l'Égypte ancienne," in C. Malamoud and J.-P. Vernant (eds.), *Le Corps des dieux*, *Le Temps de la réflexion* 7 (1986): 171–91.

Chapter 2

G. Wiet, *L'Égypte de Murtadi, fils du Gaphiphe: Introduction, traduction et notes*, Bibliothèque de l'École des Langues Orientales Vivantes 14 (Paris, 1953), pp. 82–90. A. bey Kamal, *Livre des perles enfouies et des mystères précieux: Au Sujet des indications des cachettes, des trouvailles et des trésors* (Cairo, 1907), vol. 2, esp. pp. 39 and 93–94.

The accounts of certain travelers have been conveniently published by the Institut Français d'Archéologie Orientale du Caire in a series titled *Voyageurs occidentaux en Égypte*. On travelers from the sixteenth century and later, see J.-M. Carré, *Voyageurs et écrivains français en Égypte*, vol. 1: *Du début à la fin de la domination turque (1517–1840)*, Recherches d'Archéologie, de philologie et d'histoire 5 (Cairo, 1932). See also J.-M. Vansleb, *Nouvelle Relation en forme de journal d'un voyage fait en Égypte en 1672 et 1673* (Paris, 1677), pp. 144–45.

For Giza in the nineteenth century, see *Description de l'Égypte* (Paris, 1821–29), text, vol. 5, pp. 591–674, and *Antiquités*, vol. 5, pls. 6–18; there are three views of the Sphinx on pls. 8, 11, and 12. A report on the work of Caviglia in 1817 was written by H. Salt and included in the book by H. Vyse, *Operations Carried on at the Pyramids of Gizeh in 1837*, vol. 3 (London, 1842), Appendix 3, pp. 107–14; later, Vyse investigated the pyramid of Cheops. See also R. Lepsius, *Denkmäler aus Ägypten und Äthiopien*, vol. 3 (Berlin, 1851). A. Mariette left only brief notes on his work at Giza, principally in *Le Sérapéum de Memphis: Notes additionelles* (Paris, 1882), pp. 99–100; further information can be gleaned from his correspondence.

For the beginnings of photography, see the exhibit catalogue by A. d'Hooghe and M.-C. Bruwier, *Les Trois grandes Égyptiennes: Les Pyramides de Gizeh à travers l'histoire de la photographie* (Paris, 1996).

The archives of P. Lacau, which are still largely unpublished, are kept at the Centre W. Golenischeff, École Pratique des Hautes Études, Section des sciences religieuses.

For modern studies of the Sphinx, see S. Hassan, *Le Sphinx: Son histoire à la lumière des fouilles récentes* (Cairo, 1951); idem, *The Great Sphinx and Its Secrets: Excavations at Giza 1936–1937* (Cairo, 1953); M. Lehner, "Archaeology of an Image: The Great Sphinx of Giza," Ph.D. dissertation, Yale University, 1991; C. Zivie-Coche, *Giza au deuxième millénaire*, Bibliothèque d'Étude 70 (Cairo, 1976); eadem, *Giza au premier millénaire: Autour du temple d'Isis, dame des Pyramides* (Boston, 1991); as well as a series of articles, among them Z. Hawass, "The Great Sphinx at Giza: Date and Function," *VI Congresso Internationale d'Egittologie Atti* (Turin, 1993), pp. 177–95.

Chapter 3

On the pyramids, see especially J.-P. Lauer, *Le Mystère des pyramides*, rev. ed. (Paris, 1988); I. E. S. Edwards, *The Pyramids of Egypt*, rev. ed. (London, 1993); R. Stadelmann, *Die ägyptischen Pyramiden: Vom Ziegelbau zum Weltwunder*, Kulturgeschichte der antiken Welt 30 (Mainz, 1985).

There is a summary of various opinions concerning the proposed dates for the Sphinx in S. Hassan, *The Great Sphinx and Its Secrets: Excavations at Giza 1936–1937* (Cairo, 1953), pp. 157–62. R. Stadelmann, op. cit., pp. 125–26, defends the opinion that the Sphinx dates to Cheops, who was the first king to choose the Giza plateau for his pyramid.

My treatment of the Sphinx in this chapter owes a great deal to the study by M. Lehner, "Archaeology of an Image: The Great Sphinx of Giza," Ph.D. dissertation, Yale University, 1991, and especially to his detailed description of the statue and its surroundings, with the many plans and sections that accompany it.

Chapter 4

On the notion of the Sphinx as guardian of the cemetery, see S. Hassan, *The Great Sphinx and Its Secrets: Excavations at Giza 1936–1937* (Cairo, 1953), pp. 221 ff.

On the pyramid of Chephren, see U. Hölscher, *Das Grabdenkmal des Königs Chephren*, Veröffentlichungen der Ernst von Sieglin-Expedition in Ägypten 1 (Leipzig, 1912).

On the Sphinx temple, see H. Ricke, *Der Harmachistempel des Chefren in Giseh*, Beiträge zur ägyptischen Bauforschung und Altertumskunde 10 (Wiesbaden, 1970), pp. 1–43; S. Schott, *Ägyptische Quellen zum Plan des Sphinxtempels*, Beiträge zur ägyptischen Bauforschung und Altertumskunde 10 (Wiesbaden, 1970), pp. 49–79; idem, "Le Temple du Sphinx à Giza et les deux axes du monde," *Bulletin de la Société Française d'Égyptologie* 53–54 (1969): 31–41; R. Anthes, "Was veranlasste Chefren zum Bau des Tempels vor der Sphinx?" in A. M. Abubakr (ed.), *Aufsätze zum 70. Geburtstag von Herbert Ricke* (Wiesbaden, 1971), pp. 47–58.

See M. Lehner, "Archaeology of an Image: The Great Sphinx of Giza," Ph.D. dissertation, Yale University, 1991, pp. 96–99, for an interpretation of the function of the Sphinx in the Old Kingdom; he notes our lack of knowledge of religious thought in this period, and his hypotheses are carefully formulated.

See also B. Kemp, *Ancient Egypt: Anatomy of a Civilization*, 2d ed. (London, 1993), pp. 4–5.

Chapter 5

For this chapter, see the detailed study of the evidence in C. Zivie-Coche, *Giza au deuxième millénaire*, Bibliothèque d'Étude 70 (Cairo, 1976), esp. chapters 4–7.

On the concept of pilgrimage in Egypt, see J. Yoyotte, in *Les Pèlerinages: Égypte ancienne, Israël, Islam, Perse, Inde, Tibet, Indonésie, Madagascar, Chine, Japon*, Sources Orientales 3 (Paris, 1960), pp. 19–74.

On the history of Memphis in the New Kingdom, see A. Badawi, *Memphis als zweite Landeshauptstadt im Neuen Reich* (Cairo, 1948); and C. Zivie-Coche, "Memphis," *Lexikon der Ägyptologie*, vol. 4 (Wiesbaden, 1980), cols. 24–41.

On New Kingdom foreign policy, see C.Vandersleyen, *L'Égypte et la vallée du Nil*, vol. 2: *De la fin de l'Ancien Empire à la fin du Nouvel Empire* (Paris, 1995). Among the studies on foreign deities in Egypt, one can consult R. Stadelmann, *Syrisch-palästinensische Gottheiten in Ägypten*, Probleme der Ägyptologie 5 (Leiden, 1967); and C. Zivie-Coche, "Dieux autres, dieux des autres: Identité culturelle et altérité dans l'Égypte ancienne," in *Concepts of the Other in Near Eastern Religions* (Leiden, 1994), pp. 39–80.

On the role and activities of Khaemwese, who has been called the "first archaeologist," see F. Gomaà, *Chaemwese: Sohn Ramses' II und Hoherpriester von Memphis*, Ägyptologische Abhandlungen 27 (Wiesbaden, 1973).

For the cemeteries of Saqqara, see A.-P. Zivie, *Découverte à Saqqarah: Le Vizir oublié* (Paris, 1990); and G. Martin, *The Hidden Tombs of Memphis: New Discoveries from the Time of Tutankhamun and Ramesses the Great* (London, 1991).

On the preservation of memories and traces of the past in ancient Egypt, see D. Wildung, *Die Rolle ägyptischer Könige im Bewusstsein ihrer Nachwelt*, vol. 1, Münchner ägyptologische Studien 17 (Berlin, 1969).

The discovery and excavation of the chapel of Amenophis II are summarized by S. Hassan in *The Great Sphinx and Its Secrets: Excavations at Giza 1936–1937* (Cairo, 1953), pp. 32–50.

Royal dreams are discussed by S. Sauneron, "Les Songes et leur interprétation dans l'Égypte ancienne," in *Les Songes et leur interprétation: Égypte ancienne, Babylone, Hittites, Canaan, Israël, Islam, peuples altaïques, Persans, Kurdes, Inde, Cambodge, Chine, Japon*, Sources Orientales 2 (Paris, 1959), pp. 22–32. On the concept of personal piety, see F. Dunand and C. Zivie-Coche, *Dieux et hommes en Égypte, 3000 av. J.-C.–395 apr. J.-C.: Anthropologie religieuse* (Paris, 1991), pp. 113–14.

For the discovery of the statue of Haurun, see P. Montet, *Tanis: Douze années de fouilles dans une capitale oubliée du Delta égyptien* (Paris, 1942), pp. 96–102 and pl. 4. On Ramesses' statue of Haurun at Giza, see R. Stadelmann, "Ramses II., Harmachis und Hauron," in J. Osing and G. Dreyer (eds.), *Form und Mass: Beiträge zur Literatur, Sprache und Kunst des alten Ägypten, Festschrift für Gerhard Fecht zum 65. Geburtstag am 6. Februar 1987*, Ägypten und Altes Testament 12 (Wiesbaden, 1987), pp. 436–49 and pl. 13.

On the colossi of the deified Ramesses II, which are often depicted on stelae, see L. Habachi, *Features of the Deification of Ramesses II*, Abhandlungen des Deutschen Archäologischen Instituts Kairo, Ägyptische Reihe 5 (Glückstadt, 1969), pp. 28–35.

For the existence of a cult of Isis on the plateau of Giza in the New Kingdom, see C. Zivie-Coche, *Giza au premier millénaire: Autour du temple d'Isis, dame des Pyramides* (Boston, 1991), pp. 19–42.

A brief description of the fragments of the "Osirid" statue can be found in A. Mariette, *Le Sérapéum de Memphis: Notes additionnelles* (Paris, 1882), pp. 95 and 99–100.

Chapter 6

On Memphis in the first millennium, see C. Zivie-Coche, "Memphis," *Lexikon der Ägyptologie,* vol. 4 (Wiesbaden, 1980), cols. 29–31. A fundamental study of the Third Intermediate Period, down to the Saite Dynasty 26, is K. A. Kitchen, *The Third Intermediate Period in Egypt,* 3d ed. (Warminster, 1996). For the city of Tanis, see P. Brissaud, "Tanis," in *Les Cités royales des pays de la Bible reconstitués, Les Dossiers d'archéologie* 210 (1995): pp. 47–57, and idem, "Tanis," in *L'Égypte du Delta: Les Capitales du Nord, Les Dossiers d'archéologie* 213 (1996): 66–75. Egypt's political difficulties during this period have been analyzed by J. Yoyotte, "Les principautés du Delta au temps de l'anarchie libyenne," in *Mélanges Maspero,* vol. 1, Mémoires publiés par les membres de l'Institut Français d'Archéologie Orientale du Caire 66 (Cairo, 1961), pp. 121–81 and pls. 1–3.

For a detailed and systematic study of the evidence from the first millennium, see C. Zivie-Coche, *Giza au premier millénaire: Autour du temple d'Isis, dame des Pyramides* (Boston, 1991).

The stela bearing the name of Djoser was published by P. Barguet, *La Stèle de la famine à Séhel,* Bibliothèque d'Étude 24 (Cairo, 1953). This document combines the use of the name of a venerable monarch with the literary theme of a dream during which a deity makes an appearance, as in the case of the stela of Tuthmosis IV.

On the name Harmakhis, see C. Zivie-Coche, "Bousiris du Létopolite," *Livre du Centenaire de l'IFAO,* Mémoires publiés par les membres de l'Institut Français d'Archéologie Orientale du Caire 104 (Cairo, 1980), p. 98.

On Giza in Dynasty 26, see W. El-Sadeek, *Twenty-Sixth Dynasty Necropolis at Gizeh: An Analysis of the Tomb of Thery and Its Place in the Development of Saite Funerary Art and Architecture,* Beiträge zu Ägyptologie 5 (Vienna, 1984), pp. 11–100 and 205–57.

Chapter 7

For a detailed analysis of the legend of Rhodopis, which was intertwined with that of Nitocris, see C. Zivie-Coche, "Nitocris, Rhodopis, et la troisième pyramide de Giza," *Bulletin de l'Institut Français d'Archéologie Orientale du Caire* 72 (1972): 115–38.

For the Greek texts, the translation and content of which are subject to numerous hypotheses, I have used the translations by E. Bernand, *Inscriptions métriques
de l'Égypte gréco-romaine: Recherches sur la poésie epigrammatique des Grecs en
Égypte,* Annales littéraires de l'Université de Besançon 98 (Paris, 1969),
pp. 500–25.

Index

Numbers in italics refer to photographs.

117